THE FALL OF THE HUMAN INTELLECT

A. Parthasarathy

First   Edition 2007
Second Edition 2007
Third   Edition 2008

ISBN No: 978-81-906179-1-8

Published by:
A. Parthasarathy
1A Landsend
Mumbai 400 006
India
www.vedantaworld.org

Printed by:
Vakil & Sons Pvt. Ltd.
Industry Manor
Mumbai 400 025
India

CONTENTS

PREFACE

The human species alone, none other, needs an intellect for its survival. Hence it is blessed with this wondrous equipment to think, to reason and decide its course of action through life. Not realising the vital role the intellect plays in this world, humans have ignored and neglected it to a point of grievous fault.

Intellect is not *intelligence*. *Intelligence* is acquired from external agencies which renders one well informed, knowledgeable. But that does not build, improve one's *intellect*. The intellect has to be developed by oneself. There is no plan or program in the world today to develop the human intellect. The world has been imprudent in merely promoting and procuring different branches of knowledge. And people are left with a barren intellect.

The consequences of such negligence are immeasurable. Humanity is torn apart into divisions and demarcations. It has engendered bitterness and hatred, militancy and terrorism everywhere. The human race is now becoming an endangered species threatened with extinction.

You have the capacity and the expertise to avert this crisis. Arise. Save yourselves. Save the world.

A. Parthasarathy
1A Landsend
Mumbai   400 006
India

CHAPTER I

THE FALL

The world is a beautiful phenomenon of cause and effect. There is a Reality that pervades and percolates every facet of the world making it graceful, glorious. Objects and beings have been orchestrated to bring about the melody of life. A heaven upon earth.

However, that is not to be. Desire and attachment, lust and greed has devastated the human race. The root cause for this pathetic state is the fall of the human intellect, the loss of reason and judgement. Which has led people the world over to live by a herd instinct. Hardly anyone can claim to possess an intellect to think originally, freely, independently. Consequently, a heaven has become a veritable hell.

A world of peace and bliss has now been transformed into a world of strife and struggle. The joy and happiness within human beings has turned into sorrow and misery. An alarming state brought about by the neglect of the human intellect, followed by the mind's self-centredness, selfishness.

Humanity has gone off the rails. And humanity alone can put itself back on the rails. You are the architect of your fortune. You are the architect of your misfortune. You make yourself. You mar yourself. The responsibility of redeeming the world therefore falls entirely on human beings. To set it right you need to first study the human constitution and fulfil your role as a human being.

Anatomy of Human Beings

A human being is composed of Spirit and matter. The Spirit is the Self, the divine core of the human personality. Matter comprises the body, mind and intellect. The Self enlivens the body to perceive and act, enlivens the mind to feel and the intellect to think, contemplate. However, the type of perception and action, feeling and thought emanating from the body, mind and intellect will depend upon one's inherent nature known as *vasanas*. As the *vasana* so the thought, feeling, perception and action.

The chart below gives the constitution of a human being with his built-in anatomical, physiological, psychological, intellectual and philosophical structures.

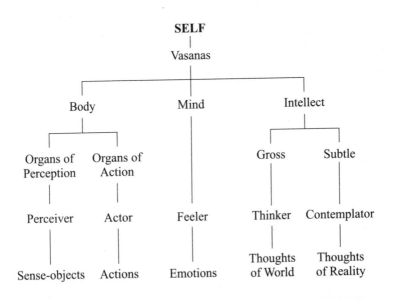

The *body* comprises the organs of perception and the organs of action. The organs of perception perceive the sense-objects of the world. Eyes see colour and form, ears hear sound, nose smells odour, tongue tastes food, skin feels touch. The Self functioning through the organs of perception becomes the *perceiver*, perceiving the sense-objects of the world. That makes up one part of the physical personality. The other part is the *actor*, created by the Self functioning through the organs of action. The actor executes action. The *actor* and the *perceiver* together form the physical personality.

Within the *body* lie two wondrous equipments known as the *mind* and the *intellect*. The *mind* is composed of feelings, emotions, likes and dislikes. The Self functioning through the *mind* becomes the *feeler*, experiencing joy, sorrow, love, hatred, passion, affection, anger, jealousy etc. The *feeler* is the emotional personality.

The third and the most important equipment in a human is the *intellect*. The *intellect* is that which thinks, comprehends, reasons, judges, decides. It is designed to guide, direct the mind and its emotions, the body and its perceptions and actions.

The *intellect* is of two types: the gross-intellect and the subtle-intellect. They execute distinct functions in human life. The gross-intellect operates within the precincts of the terrestrial world. From the simplest distinctions to the profound themes of science and technology — all fall under the purview of the gross-intellect. The Self expresses through the gross-intellect as the *thinker*. The intellectual personality conceiving thoughts pertaining to the world.

Beyond the gross-intellect lies the subtle-intellect. The subtle-intellect crosses the limits of the terrestrial world to conceive the transcendental Reality. It distinguishes the Eternal from the ephemeral. Discerns Spirit from matter. The Self expresses through the subtle-intellect as the *contemplator*. As the spiritual personality conceiving the Self which transcends the body, mind, intellect and their manifestations.

Thus a human being is a hyphenated perceiver-actor-feeler-thinker-contemplator. A synthesis of physical, emotional, intellectual and spiritual personalities. As projected in the chart below.

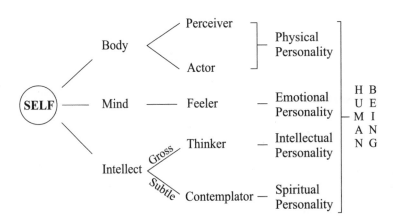

CHAPTER II

HISTORY OF HUMAN DEVELOPMENT

Human history tracing back to its origin reveals four distinct stages of human development in ascending order:

1. Age of Perception
2. Age of Observation
3. Age of Scientific Enquiry
4. Age of Contemplation.

Age of Perception

At the beginning of human existence people lived in the Age of Perception. In that Age the mass of humanity merely perceived the phenomenal world. Their organs of perception registered the sense-objects like sight, sound, smell, taste and touch. That was all. Their experience of the external world ended there with no further reaction within themselves. People in that era were content in just gazing at the outer world. It took a long, long time before humanity rose from the Age of Perception to the next Age of Observation.

Age of Observation

In the second stage of development people were not content with mere gazing at nature. They began to react within with what they perceived. That marked the beginning of the Age of Observation. In this era people's minds observed certain happenings and correlated them without intellectual discernment. It lacked reason or judgement. There was no cause and effect relationship established. They would observe two occurrences and correlate them as cause and effect. For example, a person observed a black cat crossing as he was on the way to his business. And the business happened to fail. He forthwith related these two events to believe that the crossing of the black cat brought about the failure. Thus emerged the era of superstition. An era when generations after generations lived their lives in superstitious beliefs and ritualistic practices.

They had no knowledge of the science of cause and effect. They held on to ridiculous superstitions and rituals. A practice that has caused sorrow and misery to human lives.

Age of Scientific Enquiry

Humanity slowly graduated from that spell of superstition to the Age of Scientific Enquiry. They began to visualise the vivid expressions of cause and effect everywhere. That the world is governed by the law of causation. Every cause has an effect and every effect, a cause.

In the first two Ages the intellect remained undeveloped. Human beings needed to awaken and apply their intellect to apprehend the laws that control the world. The Age of Scientific Enquiry ushered the dawn of the intellect. People began to enquire into the phenomenon of cause and effect. Their enquiry led to the emergence of science. And the scientists began to discover the laws governing the world. But their enquiry and effort was confined to the precincts of the world.

This is as far as the gross-intellect can go. It cannot reach any further. The human needs his subtle-intellect to probe into anything beyond the world. To realise the Reality that transcends all scientific enquiry and discovery. Lacking the subtle-intellect humanity lingered in the scientific era for long before entering into the Age of Contemplation.

Age of Contemplation

This is the last stage of human development. When the subtle-intellect conceives and contemplates upon the supreme, all-pervading Reality. Beyond your body and its perceptions and actions, beyond your mind and its impulses and emotions, your intellect and its thoughts lies the Reality. The human alone is endowed with the subtle-intellect which can contemplate and penetrate into the unknown Reality, referred to by the layperson as God. Reaching the transcendental State marks the acme of human existence. Hardly anyone conceives, much less attempts to attain that exalted State.

The Present Era

The above four Ages depict the gradual development of the human species. However, in today's world the four Ages seem to coexist. There are people living at the level of the body with hardly any reaction with the outside world. These are rare ones who still belong to the Age of Perception.

Others operate with the impulses of the mind and are caught up in blind beliefs, weird superstitions and ritualistic practices. A large percentage of people today falls under this category. Human beings lack intellectual application in their lives. Their intellect is virtually absent. They do not doubt or question their extreme reliance on beliefs and superstitions. And have sold their personalities to peers and authorities.

Even before people reach their adulthood, before the intellect has matured, they consider themselves atheistic or religious, Christian, Hindu or Muslim, capitalist or communist etc. On what basis do they assume these positions? There is no thought, reason or judgement supporting any one of their assumed personalities. Since the vast majority of human beings falls under the above category there are not many intellectuals today who can claim to have a scientific background.

The present era can no doubt boast of discoveries and inventions. Yet the scientific-minded intellectuals form a low percentage. Rare indeed are those who are founded on logic and reason. Who will not take things for granted. Who are not driven by doctrines and dogmas, maxims and mandates.

The modern generation can claim no more than a rare few who have reached the Age of Contemplation. Who contemplate upon the Reality. Who revel in the supreme Consciousness that pervades the body, mind and intellect. Who have attuned to the Transcendental that lies beyond the terrestrial world of perception, emotion and thought.

The present-day world is therefore an admixture of the four Ages of Perception, Observation, Scientific Enquiry and Contemplation. Those contemplating upon the Reality being so few, there is considerable pressure pulling the layperson to the lower stages. To tear apart from such peer pressure and to pursue the highest state of contemplation needs extreme intellectual effort. Every human will do well to use his subtle-intellect to the maximum capacity to contemplate upon and attain the ultimate experience of Self-realisation.

CHAPTER III

PLANT, ANIMAL AND HUMAN

The Three Species

Living creatures fall under three broad categories: plant, animal and human. They differ in their basic constitution. The plant has only a body. It has no mind to feel emotions or intellect to think, contemplate upon thoughts. Whereas, the animal has a body and mind but no intellect. Animals have likes and dislikes, feelings which is seen clearly in their relationship with their offspring and other creatures. The intellect is absent in them, though certain animals display a rudimentary gross-intellect. Like a dog distinguishing between its master and a stranger. But all animals are denied the subtle-intellect. None of them can conceive God, anything transcending the terrestrial world. Whereas, humans possess a body, mind and both the gross-intellect and subtle-intellect. A human being alone is blessed with the subtle-intellect which can entertain the thought of the Transcendental, God. Even the atheist uses his subtle-intellect to deny the existence of God.

Humanity seeks peace and progress in life. To attain that a human is equipped with the intellect. He must develop and use his intellect to control and direct his impulses and emotions, his perceptions and actions towards peace and progress. He cannot afford to let his mind's impulses directly take over his activities. His intellect must reason, judge the impulses and decide the course of perception and action. Failing which he would meet with deep trouble. The dramatist William Shakespeare has highlighted the grave blunder of humanity in acting impulsively without the guidance of the intellect. His tragedies like *King Lear, Othello, Hamlet* have shown how impulsive actions have proved detrimental, fatal. The plays ending with misery and death.

Above all, a human alone is endowed with the unique faculty of using his subtle-intellect to cross over the mire of ignorance and attain Self-realisation. Gain spiritual Enlightenment. But the sad plight of the world today is that people are unaware of the great faculty in them and none really puts in the effort to reach that exalted State.

How the Species Function

The plant kingdom ranges from banyan trees to creepers, flower-beds to weeds. They have a distinct character. They merely exist in the world at large exhibiting their nature. With no voluntary reaction to the world. No eyes to gaze at the environment around.

Animals have a built-in programme to live their lives. They cannot tamper with their natural constitution. A tiger cannot become a vegetarian nor a cow a flesh eater. Eating habits apart, the behavioural pattern of each species of animals is clearly defined by their basic nature, *vasanas*. The *vasanas* of a species determine their temperament, disposition, character which projects their particular mode of living. The creatures of each species are constituted of the same *vasanas*. They possess a collective nature. They function much the same way in accordance with their *vasanas*. All lions are ferocious. There can be no lion meek and mild. So are all deer soft and tender. And there can be no deer ferocious.

The human species stands out distinct and different from all other creatures. The nature of each human being is singular. Each one is constituted of his individualistic nature, *vasanas*. No two humans possess the same *vasanas*. Consequently, each one expresses his or her own behavioural pattern. Hence human beings have to be treated individually, not collectively as in the case of other creatures.

The behavioural pattern of animals follows their own nature. They have no choice to live apart from it. But humans are free to choose their course of life. All through life you are faced with the dilemma of choice. To get into business or profession, to marry or not to marry, to be a vegetarian or non-vegetarian etc. The problem lies not so much in making a choice but on what basis you make it. That requires a study of the forces that propel human action.

The Dilemma of Choice

Human actions emanate from either the mind or the intellect or a combination of both. The body executes action. But the body cannot act on its own.

The actions of the body are driven by either:

1. Likes and dislikes, feelings, emotions, impulses of the mind

   or

2. Reason, discretion, judgement of the intellect

   or

3. A combination of the above two.

Here is an example of the above three possibilities arising from an action. Offer a sweet to a diabetic person who is fond of sweets. His mind wants to take it. His intellect decides against it knowing that he is diabetic. If his intellect is more powerful than his mind he will refuse it. If otherwise, his mind is strong and intellect weak, he would accept it. In a third possibility, if the person is not diabetic, his mind and intellect may concur* and consume it.

People the world over operate more on feeling and emotion rather than by reason and judgement. Sometimes even the reasoning of the intellect is overpowered by the mind's emotion. Jane Taylor in her poem *The Pond* portrays this idea beautifully. The poem describes a party of ducks repairing to a pond for its food and pastime. A young chicken that lived thereabout kept watching the ducks go in and out of the water thoroughly enjoying themselves. She had a great desire to get into the pond and join in their fun and frolic. But her mother had warned her not to go into the water. One day the chicken tried to reason to herself why she should not venture into the pond despite her mother's warning. And arrived at a strange conclusion that the only difference between them and herself was in the shape of their beaks. That her beak was pointed and their beaks round. She found it to be no reason for her to drown. Thus submitting to her mind's obsession for swimming, her intellect thought she could swim as well as the ducks. So she plunged into the water only to find her mother's cautions were true. She sank to the bottom and died.

The Pond

There was a round pond, and a pretty pond too;
About it white daisies and violets grew,
And dark weeping willows, that stood to the ground,
Dipped in their long branches, and shaded it round.

A party of ducks to this pond would repair,
To feast on the green water-weeds that grew there:
Indeed, the assembly would frequently meet
To discuss their affairs in this pleasant retreat.

Now the subjects on which they were wont to converse
I'm sorry I cannot include in verse;

For, though I've oft listened in hopes of discerning,
I own 'tis a matter that baffles my learning.

One day a young chicken that lived thereabout
Stood watching to see the ducks pass in and out,
Now standing tail upward, now diving below:
She thought of all things she should like to do so.

So the poor silly chick was determined to try;
She thought 'twas as easy to swim as to fly;
Though her mother had told her she must not
go near,
She foolishly thought there was nothing to fear.

"My feet, wings, and feathers, for aught that I see,
As good as the ducks are for swimming," said she;
*"Though my beak is pointed, as their beaks are round,
Is that any reason that I should be drowned?"*

"Why should I not swim, then, as well as a duck?
I think I shall venture, and e'en try my luck!
For," said she — spite of all that her mother had
taught her —
"I'm really remarkably fond of the water."

So in this poor ignorant animal flew,
But soon found her dear mother's cautions were true;

She splashed, and she dashed, and she turned
herself round,
And heartily wished herself safe on the ground.

But now 'twas too late to begin to repent;
The harder she struggled the deeper she went,
And when every effort had vainly been tried,
She slowly sunk down to the bottom and died!

The ducks, I perceived, began loudly to quack
When they saw the poor fowl floating dead on
its back;
And, by their grave gestures and looks,
'twas apparent
They discoursed on the sin of not minding a parent.

— Jane Taylor

The poem depicts the intellect being held hostage by
the overpowering emotion of the mind. The intellect
yields to the pressure of emotion and reasons in a
circle. And one meets the fate of the chick.

In another poem *The Village Preacher*, the poet Oliver
Goldsmith shows how the human intellect should
reign over the mind's feeling and emotion. He
describes the village preacher with a heart full

of chaste emotions for his fellow-beings. But never does he let his emotions disturb his intellectual poise and judgement. His head rules over his heart. Goldsmith uses a striking metaphor to describe the grandeur of the preacher's personality. Compares him to a tall cliff that rises well above the level of the clouds. The clouds gather around the breast of the mountain. But they do not disturb the serenity of the peak. The clouds represent the emotions of the mind. The peak, the intellect. The emotions of the preacher never unsettle his intellectual awareness and decision. His intellect governs his mind. The poem concludes with this metaphor:

> *To them his heart, his love, his griefs were given,*
> *But all his serious thoughts had rest in Heaven.*
> *As some tall cliff that lifts its awful form,*
> *Swells from the vale, and midway leaves the storm,*
> *Though round its breast the rolling clouds are spread,*
> *Eternal sunshine settles on its head.*

To have emotions is a virtue. But it would be a grievous error to let them interfere with your intellectual judgement. That would tantamount to human weakness. History reveals this intellectual weakness of human beings in letting their emotions overthrow discretion and judgement.

A Herd Instinct

Few in this world think and decide one's course of action. People do what their predecessors have done with little investment of thought. You go through scholastic education because all others have done so. You join a university and pursue a degree, again following the general trend. Get into a profession or business by mere peer or parental pressure. Choose a partner without examining the reasons for a life's commitment. Beget children not realising the consequences thereof. Thus everyone goes through each facet of life without thought and reason supporting it. Just imagine, even before growing into an adult, a person asserts he is a Hindu, Christian, Muslim etc. What is the basis for such a grave assertion? Without giving the subject intellectual scrutiny and analysis everyone vehemently upholds one's creed and denounces others'. Such fanatic adherence to one's religion has caused social chaos. And the lack of intellectual application has resulted in bitterness, animosity and bloodshed to the human race.

Humans today follow a herd instinct. Like sheep following sheep, like pigeons following pigeons etc. But you notice a tiger walking all alone, an eagle soaring high in the sky all by itself. This is possible because these creatures have individual strength. So too a human being needs intellectual strength to stand on his own feet. To guide his life's course in the world. And if he does not possess a strong intellect he just follows the herd.

In July 2005 a newspaper in Turkey carried a caption **1,500 sheep take suicide leap off cliff**. The report referred to an incident in Gevas, a town in eastern Turkey, when a sheep leapt to death from a cliff. Following a herd instinct nearly 1,500 more sheep plunged into the 15 metre drop in a bizarre mass suicide. Stunned shepherds looked on helplessly as their sheep took the fatal leap.

So is the herd instinct devastating the human race. The world today is emaciated of reason and logic. Even the intelligentsia have stopped thinking. Humans have lost their dignity and grandeur and have led themselves to the dire consequence of strife and struggle, vandalism and terrorism, misery and death. Even after being driven to such extremity the world has not woken up from its intellectual slumber. The herd instinct continues.

A typical example of the lack of intellectual application is the way people treat the institution of marriage. They plunge into relationships with hardly any thought, reason or judgement backing it. Interestingly, there are six broad reasons for anyone to enter into marital relationship.

The Six Reasons:

1. Progeny All creatures except humans are compelled to act on the urge for progeny. The desire to procreate their own species is predominant in all beings. Only a human being possesses the intellect to free himself from such desire. With the lack of intellectual strength people generally succumb to the desire for progeny.

2. Possessiveness With the mind overpowering the intellect most humans entertain a sense of possessiveness. They tend to accumulate objects and beings. And develop a feeling of possessiveness towards their possessions. It manifests in their expressions of *me* and *mine* — my home, my business, my name, my fame etc. Possessiveness extends to a need for a partner in life — my wife, my husband. Few realise the dire consequences of developing the trait of possessiveness. If unattended, it leads to separation from the objects and beings of possession, causing suffering and sorrow. Nevertheless, possessiveness remains one of the reasons for courting marriage.

3. Companionship The lack of self-sufficiency in a human being manifests as his dependence on other beings. People have a general tendency to seek the company of other beings. Some seek the company of humans. Others, confronted with problems associated with human companionship, find solace in the company of pets and even plants. Thus the need for companionship is yet another reason for humans to seek life partners. Few possess the intellectual calibre to be free from the desire for companionship. Who are self-sufficient and do not require a partner in life.

4. Sex The demand for sex in a human ranges from nothing to promiscuity. Its varying strengths manifest in four ways:

a) *Impotent* This class of persons lack the urge for sex even when provoked. Such people do not need a partner for this reason.

b) *Passive* The sexual urge of this class is low. It does not manifest by itself unless provoked. Left to themselves the *passive* do not need any form of sexual encounter unless they are driven to it through provocation.

c) *Active* The urge in the *active* manifests in a regular pattern. It could range from a daily demand for sex to once in several weeks. However, it manifests without needing any external stimulus.

d) *Promiscuous* This type of persons possesses insatiable urge which manifests without any external inducement. They would require repeated sexual encounters with change of partners as well. Choosing a partner in such cases would create problems for oneself and partner.

A study of the above four classes of persons would reveal that marriage is suitable for the *active* and a section of the *passive* categories considering one's sexual requirement.

5. Protection By choosing a partner one would be protected from others making amorous advances. Thus one is in a way settled in life. This makes marriage more of a convenience. There are, of course, other means of providing oneself protection in which case marriage becomes redundant.

6. Security A partner would serve as a security in times of need for help in any form. Though considered as one of the reasons it cannot stand out for justifying marriage if the other five reasons are absent.

Rare indeed are those free from all the six reasons. Such persons alone can afford to remain single. The above analysis exposes that people are ignorant of these reasons. Much less aware of the importance of the intellectual role in committing oneself to a life partnership. People just follow the herd.

CHAPTER IV

THE MIND WREAKS HAVOC

The human mind can become ruinous if the intellect is not developed enough to govern it. The mind behaves like a child while the intellect plays the role of an adult. The child needs constant supervision by an adult. So does your mind need the attention and guidance of your intellect. An uncontrolled mind can wreck a human being. Most people invariably succumb to the pressures of the mind which has proven detrimental, even fatal.

Herein is a detailed analysis of the devastating nature of a mind ungoverned by the intellect:

Likes and Dislikes

The mind is constituted of one's likes and dislikes. Human beings are caught up in their own attractions and aversions. People act as they like and avoid what they dislike. Their conduct of life is based on their mind's preferences rather than intellect's discretion. They are carried away by the whims and fancies of the mind. Handicapped by the lack of intellectual strength and guidance.

Humans face a grave problem in the indiscriminate pursuit of their likes and dislikes. The problem stems from a strange paradox in life. Whatever experience is pleasurable in the beginning turns out to be detrimental in the end. And what is detestable in the beginning becomes beneficial, even delightful in the end. Ironically, sorrow appears in the garb of joy and joy in the garb of sorrow. As a result people yield to pleasant beginnings only to end in bitterness. And they avoid unpleasant beginnings to lose their joy of life. A few common examples expose this human weakness. People like to laze and dislike exercise. Also, they like to eat junk food and dislike health food. Their choices cause health problems later in life. The human tendency is to grab instant pleasures through indisciplined living and suffer their consequent sorrows. Few go through the rigours of discipline in the beginning of one's life and enjoy the peace and happiness it provides later.

There is yet another problem in living on likes and dislikes. The world is in a constant flux of change. It cannot always cater to individual likes and dislikes. You like summer and dislike other seasons. But the seasons will roll by. As a result you enjoy three months and suffer nine months in the year. Again, you long for the weekend. Thank God It's Friday. And you detest Monday morning. You are frustrated five days in a week. The trouble with most folks is that they live by their distinct likes and dislikes and cultivate more in their lifetime only to end up in frustration. Likes and dislikes are a part of your life. There is nothing fundamentally wrong with them. You need not avoid them. But you cannot allow your likes and dislikes to directly propel your actions. You must learn to use reason and judgement of your intellect to guide them properly to enduring peace and happiness.

Worry and Anxiety

Another disturbing attribute of the mind is worry and anxiety. The mind is worried over what has happened in the past and anxious as to what will happen in the future. That causes mental agitation and sorrow.

It is worry and anxiety that saps human energy. It tears a person apart. And you become tired and fatigued. You believe that work tires you. Work can never tire you. It is your worry and anxiety that causes fatigue. And you are unable to carry on with your business. You need stimulants like coffee to energise you during work. You need rest and recreation by the end of the day. You need a two-day break at the end of the week. A vacation at the end of the year. With all these breaks fatigue and boredom still plague you through life.

Ironically, the child is never tired or bored. Though a child is weak and an adult strong. Yet you find children effervescing with passion and action. They cannot remain quiet even for a moment. The reason for this flood of energy is the absence of worry and anxiety. Children are not worried over the past or anxious for the future. That provides them all the energy to be bustling with activity. Learn this lesson from children. Use your intellect to free yourself from worry and anxiety. That will render your life energetic and entertaining.

Desires

The mind filled with desires causes agitation, suffering and sorrow. You need to develop your intellect and use it to control, regulate and gradually annihilate the desires. Desire is the barrier between a human being and God. That explains why religions have personified desire as the devil. Christianity personifies desire as Satan. Islam as Shaitan. Buddhism as Mara. Hinduism as Asura. You have to cross this barrier to reach the ultimate state of spiritual Enlightenment.

An uncontrolled mind produces endless desires. The mind is like fire. You may feed fire with logs and logs of wood. It consumes them all and is ready for more. So is your mind insatiable. Replete with desires. All the stress that humans suffer from is but mental agitation caused by unfulfilled desires.

Desire is defined as a stream of thoughts flowing from you to the object of your desire. Desires go through several modifications. When you feed the desire and the thought-flow thickens you develop *greed, avarice*. And when your desire, greed is fulfilled and you gain what you want you are faced with *fear*. You become afraid of losing what you have gained. If however your desire, thought-flow is interrupted, intercepted by an object or being the thought-flow gets deflected. The deflected thought-current is called *anger*. Consider for example, Tom loves Elizabeth. His thoughts flow towards Elizabeth. Another suitor, John also loves her.

He intercepts Tom's thought-flow. Tom develops anger towards John. Anger therefore is a modification of desire. It can never arise unless there is an underlying desire. To overcome anger you need to control the desire creating it. As desire, greed and anger well up you get into *delusion*. Your emotions mounting up to this stage develop into *arrogance* at those below your level of achievement and *envy* at those above your level. Thus a host of emotions invades your personality.

Desires, besides developing into their modifications, also multiply in numbers like bacteria. They cause agitation and sorrow in the mind. All through life the human mind moves from desire to desire trying to find fulfilment. No sooner a desire is satisfied many others spring forth. Thus you become bound, burdened with innumerable desires.

You will have therefore to use the intellect constantly to control, guide your desires and their modifications. If you fail to do so and leave them ungoverned they could cause you grief, misery and even prove fatal.

You Know Not What You Want

Ironic as it may seem, none knows what to ask for oneself. People live in a cloud of ignorance yet they claim to know what they want in life. They believe that they can define their desire clearly. But this is not true. It can be proved that whatever be your desire is really not what you want. You are disillusioned by your own desire. A simple episode exemplifies this truth. Examine it carefully.

A bachelor possessed a desire for marriage. He had everything else in life. He was most talented, renowned, healthy, wealthy. All he wanted was a partner. That was just it. He believed his life would be complete with a wife. He was sure he needed nothing more than that. Grounded in his belief he found someone to his liking and married her. He found his fulfilment in life. They enjoyed marital bliss for months and years. Until one day the couple realised that they were not begetting a child.

The man was now possessed with a powerful desire to have a child of his own. He was desperate, miserable. The couple tried all scientific ways and means to produce a child. And succeeded at last. The wife bore a son. The man was thrilled. The fulfilment of his desire shot him to the height of ecstasy. Days and months passed by in peace and contentment. Until they found out that their son was deaf. They were shattered by the finding. He would not lie low. He explored every possibility to restore the sense of hearing to his son. His desire was finally fulfilled after a surgery. The boy could hear. The man was happy again. Years passed by until he discovered that his son was mentally handicapped. He was plunged in misery once again. His only desire then was to deliver the boy to a normal state of mind.

Now, study the chain of events. From the time the bachelor desired to marry to the time the father desired to cure his son's mental disability. The desire continued, passing through its metamorphoses. So too, the underlying desire in you never ends. A desire lures you to the pleasure of its fulfilment. But no sooner you fulfil it and the mind gains the pleasure thereof, it opens up fresh ones. The desire continues. It goes on and on. Your mind remains ever agitated and stressed with unfulfilled desires.

Analyse the episode carefully. At the very beginning the bachelor had a desire for a partner. Nothing more. Later he desired a child from the marriage. Thereafter, a desire to cure the child's deafness. Followed by the desire to restore its mental health. Does it end there? The question arises as to what exactly does he want. When he first desired a partner in life, was it just a partner that he wanted? Was it merely a wife that he desired? Was that the definition of his desire? Nay, not so. Think. When he entertained a desire for a wife, the parameter of the desire was not confined to merely acquiring a wife. He actually wanted a wife who would produce a child. Was that then the demarcation of his desire? Nay, not so. Think. When he desired a wife, he actually meant a wife who would produce a son with a sense of hearing. Was that then the boundary of his desire? Nay, not so. Think. When he desired a wife, his desire meant a lot more than that. It included a child, hearing, mental stability etc. It does not end there. Therefore, any desire that you entertain has no direction or dimension. It is endless, insatiable. Yet you believe you know exactly what you want! You seem absolutely sure, certain of the confines of your desire. You must clearly understand you know not what you want. You keep chasing your own shadow. Until you are sick and tired of it all.

So it is with life. You project your egocentric desires and run after them. You may satisfy your immediate demand. No sooner you fulfil that you project other desires. You pursue those and gain them as well. Yet other demands prop up. You grope in the darkness of your ignorance. Not knowing what you really want. You are caught up in the quagmire

43

of desires. And you remain disappointed, frustrated all through life.

Sabine Baring-Gould captures this thought beautifully in his simple poem *The Olive Tree*. The poem speaks of two hermits who planted saplings to grow olive trees. They needed olives to extract oil for their prayer. One of them prayed for rain. And the rains came down. He then felt the plant needed sunlight and prayed for the sun to shine. And the sun shone bright. Next, he asked for frost and got it too. With all his prayers granted, the plant perished. Whereas, the other hermit asked for nothing. He did all that was necessary for the plant to grow. He had no demands or desires. He left it to the general plan of nature. The plant grew into a tree and yielded olives. The poem:

The Olive Tree

Said an ancient hermit bending
Half in prayer upon his knee,
'Oil I need for midnight watching,
I desire an olive tree.'

Then he took a tender sapling,
Planted it before his cave,
Spread his trembling hands above it,
As his benison he gave.

But he thought, the rain it needeth,
That the root may drink and swell;
'God! I pray Thee send Thy showers!'
So a gentle shower fell.

'Lord! I ask for beams of summer
Cherishing this little child.'
Then the dripping clouds divided,
And the sun looked down and smiled.

'Send it frost to brace its tissues,
O my God!' the hermit cried.
Then the plant was bright and hoary,
But at evensong it died.

Went the hermit to a brother
Sitting in his rocky cell:
'Thou an olive tree possessest;
How is this, my brother tell?'

'I have planted one and prayed,
Now for sunshine, now for rain;
God hath granted each petition,
Yet my olive tree hath slain!'

Said the other, 'I entrusted
To its God my little tree;
He who made knew what it needed
Better than a man like me.

Laid I on Him no conditions,
Fixed no ways and means; so I
Wonder not my olive thriveth,
Whilst thy olive tree did die.'

— Sabine Baring-Gould

The Two Motivations

Desires manifest as two powerful motivations in life —
acquisition and *enjoyment.* You want to acquire
whatever you desire from the world. And after
acquiring you long to enjoy what you have acquired.
You build a house and enjoy living in it. You prepare a
tennis court and enjoy playing the game. Etcetera.
Propelled by these two motivations every human being
craves to acquire and enjoy more and more in the
world. He consumes his entire life chasing images of
happiness. None has found true happiness in mere
acquisition or enjoyment. Yet the chase never ends.
People are ultimately exhausted with their futile efforts
and become frustrated and unhappy.

From the very beginning of life the mind has a tendency
to acquire the wealth of the world. Yet it cannot qualify
or quantify what it wants. Even in the present, when
the mind acquires the object of its desire it forthwith
pitches up something else. This thirst for acquisition goes

on and on. The wealthiest man in the world wants more wealth. The most powerful seeks more power. The most beautiful woman would like a little more beauty. Human beings face a real problem in their minds' insatiable desire to acquire, to aggrandise and the consequent agitation and frustration. The thirst can never be quenched by sheer acquisition of whatever the mind demands. Neither can the problem be solved by suppressing the desire for acquisition. In fact, there is no taboo to acquisition. You are advised only to control, regulate the mind's indiscriminate craving for acquisition.

The second motivation is the desire to enjoy what has been acquired. Here again, there is no objection to enjoyment. You are not to refrain from enjoying what the world offers you but to restrain, control your indulgence in them. The unrestricted craving for enjoyment agitates the mind and ruins your peace. You suffer. Also, you enjoy objects or beings only when you exercise voluntary regulation and moderation. If however you do not exercise control and plunge into indiscreet indulgence in sensual enjoyment you lose the charm of it. You cannot enjoy it anymore. Unrestricted indulgence kills the enjoyment that you seek.

In truth there is no joy content in the objects and beings of the world. But it is extremely difficult, nay impossible to convince the layperson that the world cannot provide the enjoyment he seeks from it. He goes to an ice cream parlour and orders Belgian chocolate. He enjoys it. He goes to a bar and orders a peg of Blue Label Scotch and revels in it. How can he be convinced that there is no joy content in them? Yet the truth remains that none can find enjoyment in the external world.

The following example can perhaps help you examine the veracity of the statement. You sit out in the garden with your family on a full moon night. You 'enjoy' the beautiful moonlight. The uneducated believe that the moon produces light. Just think. Does the moon actually produce light? Does it have light in it per se? No, not at all. Yet some believe that the light comes from the moon. Educated as you are, you know that there is no light in the moon. Whatever arguments you put forth, the ignoramuses can never accept that there is no light in the moon. They see the light coming from the moon. They experience it. They enjoy it. So it becomes impossible for them to conceive that the moon has no light in it.

Similarly, the masses lack the wisdom to accept the truth that there is no joy content in the world. Their argument is similar. They can perceive the joy in the sense-objects. And argue that they gain enjoyment out of them. Hence they can never accept there is no joy in the external world. You may likewise hold on to your views but just ponder over the moonlight example.

Attachment

Another deadly quality of the mind is its attachment to the objects and beings of the world. Early in life the child is attached to its playthings, its toys and trinkets. And it develops possessiveness towards them. The child is excited when it receives a new toy. And sad when it loses one. The child grows up to a young person. The youth's mind then craves for wealth, name, fame, a partner etc. He desires and acquires the objects of his passion. And develops possessiveness towards them. His mind tosses him high and low. Suffers from mental agitation and sorrow. As he advances in age, the old person is possessed with worry and anxiety. His mind remains disturbed all the time. Thus the entire life of human beings is burdened with the mind's attachment and possessiveness causing sorrow and suffering.

Attachment therefore is a pernicious passion destroying the peace and harmony of the young and old.

Attachment is actually a pollution of love. When love is vitiated by self-centredness, selfishness it turns into attachment. And when attachment is free from self-centred motives it is love.

$$\text{Attachment} - \text{Selfishness} = \text{Love}$$
$$\text{Love} + \text{Selfishness} = \text{Attachment}$$

The world today is infested with attachment which passes off as love. A boy meets a girl and develops an attachment for her. He marries her and begets children. He then becomes attached to the family. He purchases a house and is attached to it. He starts a business and becomes attached to it. He earns money and is attached to it. Some, tired of material pursuits, seek spiritual solace. They become attached to their religion and spiritual masters. The mind thus binds itself to anything it contacts. The bondage produces sorrow and misery. It devastates the human race.

To avoid this self-inflicted damage, you must develop and use your intellect to protect, preserve your love. You must ensure your love does not turn sour with self-centred motives. Love produces peace and harmony whereas attachment causes distress and disharmony.

When a person develops attachment to another or an object he is bound to go through pain and suffering. It does not end there. He becomes estranged to that person, to that object of attachment. Sooner or later he would lose the relationship. The loved one would desert him, even perish. And leave the lover shattered and distressed. It is the law of nature.

There are three long English poems illustrating this law. They highlight the tragic loss of relationship when one is attached to the other. It even ends with death. *Laodamia* by William Wordsworth portrays a woman's attachment to man. Laodamia was a princess passionately attached to her husband Protesilaus, the Greek prince. Her terrible attachment resulted in the loss of their relationship and the premature death of her husband. The second poem *Andrea del Sarto* by Robert Browning shows how a husband's infatuation for the wife destroys their relationship. Andrea del Sarto was one of the greatest European painters, surpassing celebrities like Rafael and others. But his deadly attachment to his wife Lucrezia ruined his great talent and work. He ultimately lost Lucrezia in their marital relationship. The third poem *Sohrab and Rustum* by Matthew Arnold is an outstanding portrayal of attachment between father and son. Rustum, the father had a sickening obsession for his son, Sohrab. So had the son for his father. Their obsession resulted in their separation and ultimately death of the son in the prime of youth.

Study the exhaustive analysis of the devastating nature of the mind set out above. It illustrates how your mind wreaks havoc. How your personality is destroyed by one or more of the mind's corrosive phases. Your likes and dislikes can drive you up to a precipice and bring about a fall. Or your worries and anxieties drain your energy and leave you exhausted, miserable. Or your mind's uncontrolled desires and attachments, acquisitions and enjoyments ruin you. Therefore, you must develop your intellect to play its vital role in controlling and directing your mind's activity.

CHAPTER V

THE VITAL ROLE OF THE INTELLECT

Humanity has Stopped Thinking

The human race suffers from the virus of attachment and aversion, greed and envy, lust and jealousy and a host of other baneful emotions. The virus has destroyed the human intellect. Even the intelligentsia have stopped thinking, enquiring. They seem quite complacent with merely obtaining information, knowledge from external sources. The knowledge thus acquired provides them with mere intelligence. And they become informed on one or more subjects. But that does not develop one's original, independent thinking free from past influence and bias. William Shakespeare in his play *Julius Caesar* deplored the fall of the human intellect centuries back in his oft quoted declaration: *O judgement, thou art fled to brutish beasts, and men have lost their reason!* There is a dire need for human beings to develop the intellect. And use it to control, direct the mind's activity towards their resurrection.

People have lost their faculty to think, to reason. Few understand thinking, reasoning as a human prerogative. No other species is blessed with this faculty. Humans must revive it for their survival. They are not innately endowed with the ability to think clearly and logically. And they do not care to develop it. Thinking is not something that comes to you naturally like respiration or perspiration. You must devote time and effort to question, reason and build your intellect.

The problem with the lack of intellect is actually graver than it appears to be. *It is aggravated by the fact that one needs an intellect to notice the absence of intellect.* Projecting this observation to the extreme, an insane person does not know he is insane! So has the German philosopher Arthur Schopenhauer observed: *Intellect is invisible to the man who has none.* The plight of human beings is that they do not know their activities lack the support of thought, reason or judgement. The mass of humanity mechanically follows a routine pattern of life set by its predecessors. There is little investment of rationale or logic in the present mode of living. People are unaware that their lives are following a herd instinct. They do not realise the gravity of the situation. Like a person not knowing that he is suffering from a malady. To have a disease in your body is serious enough. But to have it and not be aware of it would be disastrous, even fatal. The need of the hour is to recognise this grave situation and to build the intellect. Start the process by thinking, examining and questioning every moment, every facet of life.

Result of Non-thinking

The world has lost the wondrous faculty of the intellect to think originally, independently. People are possessed with groundless beliefs and faiths. You pick them up without question or reason. Without proof of their credibility. And accept them as a matter of fact. You must realise some of your strongest beliefs had taken root in your childhood. Your life runs on those faithful lines. They seem too obvious to you that you feel it would be sacrilegious to question them.

Two children of unknown religious background were brought up in different religious environments. One by a staunch Christian family. The other by a devout Muslim family. As they grew up the former declared himself a Christian professing his Biblical beliefs. And the latter pronounced himself a Muslim professing Islamic beliefs. Both have not cared to question, analyse their validity before assuming such a solemn stand in life.

Likewise, two children of the same family brought up in two different countries adopted their respective political beliefs. The child living in the communistic environment grew up to be a communist. While the other living in a capitalistic background became a capitalist. Scarce indeed does one exercise one's thought, reason or judgement before adopting any political standing.

William Drummond wisely observes: *He who cannot reason is a fool; he who will not is a bigot; he who dare not is a slave.*

The human race has for long succumbed to fanatic faith and belief without intellectual assessment and evaluation. Such irrational approach to life bereft of logic and reason has led humans to perennial strife and struggle, antagonism and terrorism all over the world.

The loss of intellect and its application to life has caused the fungus of pseudo-religious and psychic bodies to spread everywhere. Resulting in astrologers and soothsayers, *vaastu-shastris* and feng shui-ers proliferating and destroying the dignity and grandeur of the human race. The world has reached a tragic state where such pseudo-practices are flourishing while the true human culture is fast perishing.

Humanity is blatantly ignorant and pays no attention to the most essential aspect of human development — building the intellect. The modern generation assesses a person only through his scholastic education and overt behaviour. Much time and effort is devoted to language, grammar and construction. And all emphasis is on information, knowledge and technology acquired from external sources. None sees the importance, nay the necessity to *think* clearly, correctly. To develop the art and skill of *thinking*. Self-appointed educators today lack the fundamentals of education. They are unaware of their limitation to think originally. But the problem lies not in their ignorance but their firm belief that they know what they really do not. Josh Billings brilliantly conveys this idea: *The trouble with most folks is not so much their ignorance, as their 'knowing' so many things which ain't so.*

You need to wake up from this slumber. Start thinking, questioning, enquiring as to the cause of all this strife and struggle. Examine the truths of life. Do not accept anything without reason and logic. Apply your intellect to verify their authenticity. Whatever complies with the principles of sound judgement, learn to accept them. Apply them in your life. You will then taste the joy of higher and chaster living. That would usher peace and harmony in the world.

Humans have lost this fundamental principle of education. Few understand that knowledge proceeds from the known to the unknown. An unknown entity can be known only through known factors. And not through other unknown factors. Consider, the origin of the world. It is unknown. People question, enquire as to the origin. The answer given to them is that 'God' created the world. God is declared to be the origin of the world. This is no answer. For 'God' too is unknown to humanity. How can one unknown factor convey the knowledge of another unknown factor? For example, you enquire the location of your friend's house. You do not know where it is. Your friend gives you several landmarks to locate his place. But all of them are unknown to you. They cannot help you find his house. You need at least one known landmark to locate it. So too, the unknown God is described by other unknown names and terms. That God is infinite love, infinite mercy, infinite power etc. But few realise that the human intellect cannot conceive infinity. These unknown terms cannot give you the knowledge of God. But with the loss of intellect humanity has blindly accepted these 'definitions' of God. Thus in the darkness of ignorance the self-styled religious bodies thrive, leading human beings to utter confusion and chaos. The intelligentsia who have become conscious of their limitation have given up their pursuit of God. The ignoramuses believe that they 'know' and mislead innocent masses.

The world needs to build a think tank to guide the rest of humanity. A state of emergency has been created by hosts of militant non-thinkers. And humans have become an endangered species. The critical need of the hour is to salvage the residual thinkers. Get them together and launch on a massive programme to revive the art, skill, technique of original thinking and reasoning. People need to carefully rehabilitate, rebuild their fallen intellect. A sound intellect alone can face and overcome this threatening situation created by humans. With reconstituted intellect the new generation of thinkers must reflect upon the eternal truths laid down by ancient savants and sages. Experiment and verify the authenticity of these truths in practical life and build their conviction. With such conviction they must communicate the solemn truths to save humanity from the brink of extinction.

Role of Faith

There is a general misconception that intellectuals ignore the importance of faith. It is not so. Faith has a distinct role to play in human life. In truth, humanity cannot survive without the element of faith. That you are the son or daughter of your parents is built and sustained through faith. When you sit in an aircraft you have faith that the pilot will take you to your destination. As you prepare yourself for a surgery in a hospital you have faith in the surgeon operating on you. Etcetera. These cases and countless others in your life rest on faith. But then, it is not blind faith. You cannot dismiss them as unfounded beliefs. They are no doubt belief or faith but several corroboratory evidences go together to support their credibility.

There are two brilliant definitions of faith. One by the Christian mystic Joel Goldsmith and the other by the Bengali poet of India, Rabindranath Tagore. Goldsmith defines faith as: *A belief in a thing I do not know until I come to know what I believe in.* Tagore poetises: *Faith is the bird that feels the light and sings while the dawn is still dark.* These two definitions have well captured the concept of faith.

The closest word for faith in Indian language is *shraddha*. But *shraddha* encompasses more than mere faith. In *shraddha*, the mind starts with faith in something but it does not end there. The intellect thereafter pursues it until it is assimilated, made one's own. For example, a person may have faith in God but not be truly spiritual. But *shraddha* makes him pursue spiritual truths, study and reflect upon them until he is transformed into a divine person. With faith you gain mere *knowledge* of a subject. While *shraddha* provides you with *wisdom* to live it. When your intellect examines, reflects upon the knowledge gained, it metamorphoses into wisdom. Knowledge provides you with information. Wisdom brings about your transformation.

Objectivity in Life

There is a dire need for humanity to break through its herd instinct and start thinking originally. To put in your effort to overcome the environmental influence of the past and learn to reflect, contemplate afresh. Get over your passive, impulsive behaviour. Apply your intellect to overpower your emotional attachment, involvement in the affairs of the world both material and spiritual. At every turn of life let reason and judgement guide all your activities. Do not sell your personality to elders, preachers or authorities. You do not have to accept tradition because it is handed down through generations. Nor follow past practices or for that matter anything just because it is spoken of or written about by several people over and over again. Instead, carefully examine and analyse the truths of life. And whatever admits your logic and reason accept it and live by it. That spells objectivity in life.

When you begin to live objectively your mind remains peaceful and happy in and through the fluctuations of the external world. Whatever happens in the outer world does not disturb your inner composure. Theodore Tilton drives home this idea succinctly in his poem *Even This Shall Pass Away*. The poem portrays the King of Persia living with perfect mental composure in all walks of life. Objective and detached, he remains equanimous through the best and worst of experiences. He understands that the world is ever in a flux of change. It goes through profit and loss, heat and cold, joy and sorrow, honour and dishonour — an endless chain of opposites. None of them stays indefinitely. Each passes away yielding to the opposite. The king in the poem displays an amazing power of witnessing these pairs of opposites without getting mentally involved in them. He refuses to identify with either the pleasant or the unpleasant. With a perfect sense of detachment he observes objectively each of them come and go. He would have nothing to do with them. Not jump with joy when good fortune visits him. Nor sink with sorrow when misfortune takes its turn. He remains unperturbed in the ever changing world with his intellectual stance: *Even This Shall Pass Away.*

The pairs of opposites constituting the world are known as *dvandvas.* The human intellect can rise above the influence of the *dvandvas.* The more you develop and apply your intellect the less would their impact be upon you. And the more peaceful you become.

The world is thus undulated with ups and downs. When your intellect is not developed enough you ride on its surface. And your mind is lacerated by undulations. You suffer from their knocks and shocks. All creatures, except humans, live on the surface of the world. They lack the intellectual ability to rise above it. Consequently, they are affected by its ruggedness.

So do the humans who do not use the intellect. They merely enjoy, cherish the brighter side of the world. And suffer, even perish in its darker side. They are victimised by environment and circumstance, trial and tribulation of the outer world. They have not developed the intellect sufficiently to rise above the mundane challenges and remain unaffected by them.

However, a human being alone is designed to free himself from the influence of the changes occurring in the world. Stand firm like a lighthouse as the waves of challenges kiss its feet and recede. He can develop a powerful intellect to rise well above the onslaughts of the rigorous world. While others lacking intellectual power and strength are like neglected boats tossed about by the waves.

Animals, deprived of an intellect, are completely victimised by the rigours of the world. Humans need not suffer thus since they possess an intellect. You must make good use of it and liberate yourself. With the development of the intellect you will be gradually relieved from the mundane pressures. However, depending upon the effort put in by individuals, their intellects rise to different levels. Akin to the flight of birds. The chicken flies. The pigeon flies. So does the eagle. But their flights are not the same. The chicken can hardly lift itself off the ground. The pigeon can rise up to a height. While the eagle soars high in the sky. Likewise, a poor intellect can hardly help a person detach and relieve himself from worldly entanglements. A more developed intellect lifts him off the gross entanglement but he still finds it difficult to withstand the impact of the ever changing world. Whereas a highly developed intellect soars far above the mundane variations and alternations, keeping him in perfect peace and tranquillity.

When your intellect is not fortified you are at the mercy of your mind. Hence, you need to ascertain the state of your intellect and strengthen it. A simple observation of your person will help evaluate your present condition. Just consider, you have lost your pen. You believe you have left it in your friend's house. Would you worry about it and call your friend? Or, your pen is with you but your watch is missing. What is the loss of a watch to you? Let's say, pen and watch are with you but you do not find your car in the parking lot. How would you take the loss of your car? If the car also is intact and you drive back home to find your fully paid house gutted, burnt to ashes. How is that? Say, your house also is perfect but on reaching there you hear your family has met with a fatal accident. How would you take that?

Now, examine the above experiences with reference to your person. That would help indicate the state of your intellect. If the slightest loss upsets you, it shows your intellect is in a poor condition. As you are able to withstand greater losses it proves that your intellect has developed strength and objectivity. Imagine the worst tragedy does not make the slightest difference in you. You remain unperturbed, calm and composed. And you go about normally pursuing your actions and obligations in the world. You can achieve that state when your intellect soars high and maintains perfect objectivity in life. You then command enduring peace and happiness.

How to Relate to the World

People round the globe are unaware that every human being is governed by his own distinct, singular nature. Hence they do not know how to relate to other humans and suffer endless trial and tribulation. But with respect to other creatures they understand that each species possesses the same nature and relate to them accordingly. They would feed a deer in a zoo but not a lion. They would keep their distance from a cobra but pick up a kitten and fondle it. Because they understand and expect all creatures to behave according to their collective nature. Whereas they expect, even demand, a human to behave different from his particular nature. The layperson therefore knows how to relate to all other creatures except human beings. He has no problem in dealing with other species. But he has problems relating to humans. Makes blunders and suffers from stress.

The divorce rate among couples in most developed, advanced countries has reached alarmingly high levels. Parents have constant confrontation with their children. Colleagues in offices clash with each other. Communities everywhere are torn apart. The cause for this sad state of affairs is the lack of individual assessment of humans. People do not study and determine the nature of persons individually and expect one to behave different from one's basic structure. Like expecting a lion to behave like a deer or vice versa. You commit the grave blunder of not assessing each person and want him to behave different from his specific nature. You want the world to fit into your frame of mind. That is just not possible. You cannot expect people to behave according to your mental pattern. Not realising this you keep complaining, grumbling about the world around you. There is a wise saying: *All grumbling is tantamount to, 'Oh! Why is the lily not an oak?'*

To avoid such consequences and to live in peace and harmony humans must carefully examine the world around them. Individually assess the persons you contact. Find out each one's inherent nature and behavioural pattern. Start with those closest to you. Like your spouse, your children, your colleagues in office. Those whom you contact daily. You must clearly discern their basic constitution. What type of innate tendencies, *vasanas* that constitute each person. Expect one to behave according to one's particular nature. And understand that every human helplessly manifests his own nature. As you do yours.

Likewise must you evaluate, assess everything around you. Like the weather, the environment, the society, the government etc. you live in. If something is wrong and can be corrected you may do so. If however it is not possible to correct it you must learn to live with it. You then cannot expect things different from what they actually are. If you do, you will feel disappointed and stressed.

A true episode that took place in Chennai, India in 1939 drives home this point. It was a humid day in summer when the temperature had shot up to 44° Celsius. The students in a classroom were all fussing about the scorching heat. The teacher saw them disturbed by the heat as he entered the classroom. Instead of sitting at his desk he crossed over to an open quadrangle and beckoned the students to come out. He stood under the blazing sun as the students wondered what was happening. He suddenly threw up his arms and exclaimed, "Isn't this a beautiful summer?" The boys could not relate to what he said. He continued, "The beauty of the summer is its heat. The beauty of the winter is its biting cold. The beauty of the monsoon is that it must pour and pour. But the problem with you all is that you want the summer to be cold, the winter to be warm, the monsoon to be dry!" He did not stop at that. He exemplified further, "The beauty of the African is his dark skin. The beauty of the Englishman is his fair skin. But the African wants to be fair. The Englishman wants to be tanned." This madness goes on and on. People are unreasonable in expecting something different from the original nature of an object or being. These unreasonable expectations cause mental agitation, frustration, stress everywhere.

Therefore, you must learn and look at persons, beings and things, environments and situations as they are and not what you would like them to be. You would then be able to appreciate the beauty in everything, everybody, everywhere. At office you will admire the foul temper in your boss! At home, you will adore the nagging of your spouse!

Initiative versus Incentive

The intellect plays a vital role in your business. Sans intellectual governance the mind functions through like and dislike, desire and anger and other emotions. The pressures of the mind destroy your objectivity in action. Resulting in loss of efficiency and productivity in your field of action. You need a well-developed intellect to control the vagaries of the mind and direct it to your optimum output in life.

The knowledge acquired through academic resources only qualifies you to work in the particular field of action you are engaged in. But that does not help you overcome the mind's distraction and interference with work. Your work continues to be led more by feeling and emotion rather than reason and judgement. The intellect hardly plays its role. And the work turns out to be unproductive, even detrimental.

Hence you must constantly employ your intellect to circumvent the mind's negative influence upon your activity. To achieve this you need to fix an ideal in life.

An ideal represents your mission, goal beyond your self-centred, selfish interests. You begin by questioning, investigating the nature of your interest in the actions you undertake. What are you working for? Is it only for the welfare of yourself and your immediate family? Or does your interest go beyond the family unit to cover the wellbeing of your society? Or stretches more to embrace all humanity? Or even beyond to envelop all living creatures? The larger the circle of your dedication and service, the greater the ideal. Those who pursue their ideal develop an *initiative* to work. It gives them the energy and enthusiasm to enjoy their business.

Opposed to such noble work culture, people the world over have adopted a self-centred, selfish attitude in their activity. The business community has no concept of service or sacrifice. Consequently, there is no *initiative* within oneself to work in any field. Thus sprang the necessity to introduce *incentives* for drawing people to work. This step is hardly a solution to promote business. It is actually an unhealthy practice which diminishes work output as the workers get neutralised to enhanced pay and perk. Incentives thereafter cease to promote work as opposed to the untiring initiative to achieve their ideals.

Moreover, incentives increase the self-centred and selfish desires among workers. And the proliferation of personal desires proves cancerous to the organisation. That explains why giant companies and corporations have caved in. This problem cannot be solved by immediately discontinuing incentives. It has to be tackled carefully by first introducing the concept of working for an ideal. The employees would then develop the initiative to work for a higher cause. The emergence of initiative among employees should gradually displace the suicidal corporate practice of extracting work through incentives.

For generations, people with misled minds long for rewards without paying the price for them. They look for quick fixes. Rare indeed are those who conceive anything beyond short-term gains. Who would put in adequate effort to achieve their goals. Instead, people employ unnatural means to gain their ends. Thus arose the liberal use of fertilisers everywhere for imaginary, unreal growth. Incentives act in much the same way as fertilisers.

The modern agriculturists use chemical fertilisers to boost the growth of plants. As a result, the vegetables appear healthy but lose their nutritional value and taste. While medical practitioners prescribe vitamin tablets to fertilise human bodies. Following the same trend the corporate gurus have been indiscriminately using incentives to fertilise actions! They are unaware of the process of developing the initiative among employees to serve and promote their organisations. This unfortunate practice adopted by indiscreet management bodies has ruined the work culture. Resulting in the fall of huge corporations.

The reason for the failure of incentives in business is due to their diminishing value. No doubt the introduction of incentives to workers initially boosts their action and production. But then the effect does not stay long. It gradually fades away. And the employees lose their drive to work. The loss of their interest and enthusiasm is made up by alluring them with further incentives. Thus the blunder is repeated until they are sick and tired of work. And production comes to a grinding halt.

The problem with the use of incentives is that it is addressed to the mind. As opposed to initiative created by the intellect. The mind's demands are insatiable. The corporations, misguided by consultants, have been feeding the mind's demands liberally. And they helplessly watch the effect diminishing to nothing. A point of neutralisation experienced by the workers.

On the contrary the initiative to work can be increased by the intellect pitching up higher and higher ideals. The work then diverges to greater dimension instead of it converging to zero.

The 3 C's to Success: Concentration, Consistency, Cooperation

Productivity in business, success in any endeavour requires continual intellectual application to three disciplines viz. *concentration, consistency* and *cooperation*. They are the rudiments of achievement in any field of activity. These words are no doubt used liberally among management personnel but few really understand, much less put them into actual practice. And the use of incentives can in no way substitute the fundamental principles governing production and success.

You gain *concentration* when your mind is with your action. The mind has a natural tendency to worry over the past or become anxious of the future. You need a developed, strong intellect to focus your mind on the present job. *Concentration* is the technique exercised by the intellect to hold the mind on the present occupation without allowing it to slip into the past or future. It is measured by the extent to which the intellect manages to hold the mind in the present.

The second discipline, *consistency* is the skill of directing your actions towards the ideal, goal set to achieve. *Consistency* is impaired by the ramblings of the mind. As you work towards the goal the mind slips into other attractions. The actions then do not flow in the direction of the set goal. Herein, your intellect plays a significant role to keep all actions moving towards it. When your intellect channelises actions in the set direction you gain *consistency*. The practice of *consistency* lends power, energy, strength to action. You observe this clearly in nature. Water flowing in one direction has power. Wind blowing in one direction has power. So does light focussed in one direction. Similarly, if your actions are channelised in one direction, they become powerful. It is the mind, drawn by other attractions, that loses its direction and consistency in action. The intellect alone can control the mind and direct the actions towards the goal. When the actions flow thus there is power and success in any endeavour.

The third discipline is *cooperation*. To achieve an objective you need the *cooperation* of others. It is difficult to be an achiever in life without the spirit of cooperative endeavour. Germany and Japan were devastated in the last World War. But the citizens pooled their efforts cooperatively to rebuild their nations. Thus sprang the two nations to power and strength, both economically and politically. America and Australia were virtually nothing a little over two hundred years ago. The early settlers had also to pool their resources in a spirit of cooperative endeavour to build a nation. And have become powerful nations of the world. Hence the third essential requirement for success is met when the intellect maintains a true spirit of *cooperation* among one and all concerned.

An individual or organisation following the above three disciplines shall command success and productivity, progress and peace in any field of endeavour.

CHAPTER VI

INTELLECT VERSUS INTELLIGENCE

The crux of the problem that humanity faces today is the failure to distinguish the *intellect* from *intelligence*. Even the educated are ignorant of the exact nature of the *intellect*. Much less do they realise the importance of its role in human life. And educators the world over have been focussing all their attention and effort in merely building *intelligence*. They have invested little thought or effort in developing the *intellect*. Consequently the human intellect remains completely neglected.

Intellect is Not Intelligence

Intelligence is built in an individual by gaining information, knowledge from external sources. From teachers and textbooks, from schools and universities and other information bureaux. Using those sources you become informed, knowledgeable, even brilliant in one or more subjects that you take up. Just think for a while. Try to understand what you have achieved. The *intelligence* that you have gained provides you with the means to make a living. No more. All creatures, save humans, need no education to make a living. The carnivores and herbivores are naturally provided with this expertise. So are birds in the sky or fishes in the ocean. The human species alone requires some form of education to sustain itself. With knowledge acquired from external sources you only come up to the level of animals. Education has deteriorated to such an extent.

Distinct and different from *intelligence* is the *intellect*. Any amount of *intelligence* gained cannot per se build your *intellect*. *Intelligence* is acquired by you from external agencies much like data fed into a computer. All the information stored in a computer does not enable it to function independently. It cannot use that knowledge on its own. Likewise, you cannot use the knowledge gained without the help of your *intellect*. You need the *intellect* to think, plan and programme your life with the available knowledge. In the case of all other species save human, they are provided with a built-in programme of life. Their lifestyle is fixed. They cannot live apart from their inherent nature. So they do not need to plan and programme their lives. They can do without an *intellect* to guide them moment to moment.

The *intellect* is the faculty to think, to reason, to judge, to decide on the pros and cons of life. The capacity to question, enquire and not to take anything for granted. You will have to develop your *intellect* all by yourself. No external agencies can achieve that for you. Do not blindly follow the line of your predecessors. Instead, build the strength of your own intellect. You can achieve that by using your ability to think, to reason, to question everything you meet in life. Do not accept anything which does not admit logic or reason. The constant exercise of thinking, reasoning, questioning all through your life would strengthen your intellect. Galilei Galileo, often referred to as the father of modern astronomy, wondered why humans have discarded this wondrous faculty they possess: *I do not feel obliged to believe that the same God who has endowed us with sense, reason and intellect has intended us to forego their use.*

Intelligence Does Not Develop Intellect

The capacity to absorb fresh knowledge is called *udaana*. This capacity is maximum at infancy. And it diminishes gradually as you grow older. In the passage of life this process of absorption helps you gain information, knowledge, *intelligence*. But the *intelligence* acquired does not make you think freely, originally, reason independently. *Udaana* will not build the *intellect*. There is no cause and effect relationship between *intelligence* and *intellect*. *Intelligence* per se will not enrich the *intellect*. Ironically, the entire focus throughout the world is to gain *intelligence* while the *intellect* remains poor as ever, undeveloped. Today it is all *intelligence*, no *intellect*.

That explains why out of millions of doctors turned out by medical schools only a few have proved to be outstanding, extraordinary in their research and findings. Who have discovered life-saving drugs or subtle techniques to transplant organs in a human body. So too out of countless engineers graduated from engineering schools only a few have produced wonders like the Panama Canal, Golden Gate Bridge or Euro Channel Tunnel. In the field of law again there are but a few prodigious lawyers who overshadow even the most reputed ones. The difference arises in the strength of *intellect* in the former which the latter, possessing abundant knowledge of law, lacks. To cite an example: In Chennai, India over seventy years back, the High Court was deciding a famous case on forgery.

The lawyer defending the accused made an elaborate presentation covering practically all points of law. And when the opponent lawyer's turn came up, he requested the judge to merely put up the original document against the light.

He beseeched, "Do you see a watermark in the document, my Lord?"
The justice cooperated, "Yes, I do see an elephant watermark."
The lawyer rejoined, "This paper was manufactured in 1932."
And the original document was dated 1930! Of course, he had earlier obtained the proof of it.

The above observations demonstrate the power of a developed *intellect* vis-à-vis *intelligence*, a mere stockpile of knowledge. All the *intelligence* that people carry without the *intellect* to apply it in life tantamounts to gold bars on a mule's back. Again, *intelligence* acts like the horsepower in a car. And *intellect*, the steering wheel which controls and directs it. You will do well to make sure you have a power steering!

The faculty to think, to reason is a human prerogative. All other beings lack this faculty since they do not possess an *intellect*. The *intellect* renders a human being the chef d'ouevre of creation. But the world is unaware of this unique status. And people do not care to develop this life-saving, life-sustaining, life-surpassing equipment, the *intellect*.

Also you fail to realise that thinking, reasoning is skilled work. That you need to learn and practise. Like playing the violin or golf. You believe that thinking is a natural process like seeing, hearing or breathing. That you can think clearly, precisely without putting in the necessary effort on your part. You must understand that to develop the faculty of thinking, reasoning you need to devote as much time and effort to it as you would to learning any other art or skill.

Need to Develop Intellect

For a long period of time there has been no awareness or endeavour by humans to develop the art of thinking. As a result the lives of people are based on groundless beliefs. And their beliefs rest on some absurd superstitions. Or mere assertions which bear no proof. And now they find it difficult to question their veracity.

Following this trend humanity has reached a perilous state. People must wake up. Realise the emergent need to develop, strengthen the *intellect*. The process of thinking should have started from an early age. Having failed to do so, at least start the process now. Develop the art of thinking. Follow it up with the study of the impeccable truths of life. Delve deep into the truths. Accept those that appeal to logic and reason. Apply them in practical living. Adopt this procedure all through life. It will enable you to build your intellect. Nobel laureate Albert Einstein has observed: *Intellectual growth should commence at birth and cease only at death.*

Humans need a strong intellect to exercise the right choice of action in life. The world presents endless trials and tribulations. The human species alone is provided with an intellect to fight against and surmount mundane challenges. All other species, devoid of intellect, are helpless victims of the rigours of the external world. A powerful intellect helps humans overpower these onslaughts. But the role of the human intellect does not end there. Far above its suzerainty in the world the intellect has the unique capacity to even transcend the world and reach the ultimate state of spiritual Enlightenment. No other creature save humans can conceive, much less achieve that exalted state. You must make good use of the intellect to attain this very purpose of human birth.

Unaware of the dire need to build the intellect, people entertain themselves with merely reading others' periodicals and publications. They indulge in the mere length of study. Just poring over pages of literature apathetic towards the message therein or its deeper implications if any. Rare indeed are the ones who go into the depth of study. Thus little is assimilated, absorbed by the readers. People have been mere educated robots for generations. And have been traversing through life without knowing the meaning and purpose of it. Like mariners who sail through the seven seas without fathoming the depth below. But the rare one who cares to know, drops the plumb line anywhere and instantly finds the depth. So too, one must use the intellect to go into the depth of one's life to claim to be truly educated. It is the vertical and not the horizontal line of study that matters in life. Herbert Spencer, a thinker and writer, was one such truly educated luminary. Someone had asked him if he was a voracious reader. He instantly quipped: *No sir, if I were as big a reader as others, I would have been as big an ignoramus as others.*

The world abounds in personalities with one-sided development. *Intelligence* and no *intellect*. An example of one such person suffering from this human imbalance is a renowned scientist. He is an alcoholic and his liver is damaged. He is extremely short-tempered and his blood pressure has shot up. And he is stressed, unable to face even the petty challenges of the world. Just reflect over his state. Analyse his personality carefully. He is a brilliant scientist with profound knowledge of his subject. He has acquired abundant *intelligence* but never cared to develop his *intellect*. His intellect has always remained weak. It lacks the strength to handle the multifarious demands of the mind. His mind craves for alcohol. His intellect is not powerful enough to control the nagging desire. So too his mind raves in foul temper. His poor intellect is unable to control its ravings. And when his mind is humiliated, strained and stressed by the problems confronting it, his frail intellect looks on helplessly.

On the contrary, there are luminaries possessing awesome intellects which hold their minds under perfect control. Some of them possess no academic qualification but academies are built around them.

Educational institutions therefore need to maintain an equable balance between acquisition of *intelligence* and developing an *intellect*.

CHAPTER VII

THE BANE OF THE EDUCATIONAL SYSTEM

The educational systems the world over must be held responsible for the debacle of the intellect. Education has long been in the hands of those lacking true education. Institutions of learning have hit an all-time low. They need to be revamped. Further loss of time would lead the decadent human species to virtual extinction.

There are certain fundamental issues governing the principles of education. They have to be examined and introduced discreetly without upsetting the current systems.

Mode of Education

The word *educate* is derived from Latin. It means 'to draw out.' Etymologically education therefore is drawing out. Schools and universities throughout the world do not follow this basic principle of education. Knowledge has to be drawn out of students. Not thrust into them. Students would need time to pause, think, analyse the information inputs to digest them. Knowledge acquired this way stays with them. It becomes their own. But the present educational systems merely focus on feeding information from extrinsic sources. With no provision for the students to pause, reflect and examine its intrinsic worth. Information thus imposed lasts for a while and passes away. It does not register in the students. True education therefore requires one to draw out the knowledge from within using the intellect. That would mean educating gradually, carefully through questioning and trying to elicit answers from the student body. A liberal use of question and answer sessions would prove the most effective way in communicating knowledge. Alvin Toffler, the American writer and futurist, remarked: *The illiterate of the 21st century will not be those who cannot read and write but those who cannot learn, unlearn and relearn.*

Liberal and Servile Education

In the late nineteenth century John Henry Cardinal Newman authored a book in England entitled *The Idea of a University*. In which he deplored the state of the then universities. The quality of education had deteriorated to an alarming level. To highlight the damage done to education Newman had used two terms *liberal* and *servile* to define the right and wrong mode of education respectively.

He classifies education as *servile* which has a utility tag attached to it. The thought of utility while seeking knowledge, the idea of using knowledge for any vocational, mercenary or pecuniary purpose makes learning *servile*. Modern educational systems are saturated with the idea of utilisation. Different branches of knowledges have been introduced with the sole purpose of raising the standard of living. Consequently, human beings have turned sour with gross self-centredness, selfishness. This is the death knell of learning and education, wisdom and culture of the human race.

The world has lost the beauty and grandeur of *liberal* education. An education uncontaminated with utilitarian motives. Liberal education of any subject, even technical knowledge like engineering or medicine, is undertaken for education's sake, for merely acquiring that knowledge without the stigma of trading with it. Just study for study's sake. Acquire knowledge for knowledge's sake.

Liberal knowledge is knowledge which is its own end. Sufficient in itself and apart from every external and ulterior objective. A knowledge impregnated by reason. Reason is the principle of that intrinsic knowledge. Which dispenses with the necessity, for those possessing it, to look abroad for any end to rest upon external to itself. Newman thus endorses the role of the intellect in education: *Liberal education, viewed in itself is simply the cultivation of the intellect, as such, and its object is nothing more or less than intellectual excellence.*

The Cardinal's extraordinary observation and advice was a cry in the wilderness. It had little effect on the academic structure. And the quality and texture of education deteriorated further. The custodians of education and academic systems have been victims of *servile* education for a long period of time. And the human intellect has remained neglected all along. In the turn of the twentieth century the educators had emboldened themselves to advocate the cause of utilitarian education. The erstwhile education secretary in the British Cabinet, Charles Rodway Clarke has overshot himself by further contaminating the sacred institution of learning with servility.

In the Sunday Times, London May 11, 2003 Jonathan Calvert had reported on Clarke under the title *Verily, Mr Clarke, You do Play the Fool*, "The education secretary thinks academic study for its own sake is medieval, and degrees should be more utilitarian." According to the Times Higher Educational Supplement, Clarke had addressed a meeting at University College, Worcester arguing that higher education should be given state funding only if it had 'clear usefulness'!

Clarke is quoted to have said, "Education for its own sake is a bit dodgy. The idea that you can learn about the world sitting in your study just reading books is not quite right. You need a relationship with the workplace." Whatever the truth, he had reopened the debate about how much modern study should be geared towards work and the economy. Others followed his lead and challenged the worth of study for study's sake. The Confederation of British Industry had released a survey of more than two hundred firms which concluded that universities should be more 'business friendly.'

It is demeaning, nay vulgar, to look at education as a wealth creation process. Nevertheless, Clarke believed that universities should justify state funding through their benefits to the national economy doing battle in the global market. Had Clarke, the guardian of educational resources in England, been liberally educated he would have perceived the danger, in Oscar Wilde's words, of the man knowing the price of everything and the value of nothing.

The world now faces the dilemma of choosing between the sound tenets of *liberal* education based on logic and reason or continuing the baseless course of *servile* education. The choice will determine the return of human sanity or a debacle of human society into bitterness, militancy and terrorism.

Knowledge versus Wisdom

A person gains knowledge as he acquires information from external sources. The world is replete with information hunters, knowledge seekers. Who merely gather thoughts and ideas from others and become well informed on one or more subjects. They become storehouses of knowledge with little capacity to convert it to any practical use on their own. People find it difficult, if not impossible, to live by the knowledge acquired. Human beings face this perennial problem of knowing many things but unable to implement them in life. They have the *knowledge* but not the *wisdom* to graft it into their living. This has been the cry of many great souls. Rabindranath Tagore, the Nobel laureate of India, avers: *The world is full of sound scholars but not sound men.*

The problem with human beings is therefore not their ignorance of what is right and wrong in life. Practically everyone knows the right from the wrong. Good from bad. You understand what course of action you should adopt in life and what to avoid. Yet you would knowingly choose the wrong path detrimental to you and abstain from what you know is rightful and beneficial. This paradoxical behaviour arises when your *knowledge* has not matured into *wisdom*. With *knowledge* you understand and appreciate whatever. While *wisdom* enables you to live by it. It is essential therefore to convert your *knowledge* into *wisdom*. You can do it by the process of reflection known as *manana*. Your intellect must cogitate, reflect over and over upon the knowledge acquired until you digest, absorb it. Make it your own. The information you receive from external agencies must bring about your internal transformation. Then alone does *knowledge* metamorphose into *wisdom*. You then begin to live that knowledge. Educational institutions are unaware of this vital role of reflection on the part of the students receiving knowledge. Consequently, there is no provision in any institution for students to reflect upon the subject and make it their own.

Intellect over Intelligence

The world has been ignorant of the significant distinction between *intelligence* and *intellect*. The difference between mere storage of knowledge procured from others and the development of one's ability to think, judge and decide. Educational institutions everywhere commit the blunder of merely providing knowledge without attempting to develop the fallen intellect. The problem is that they do not realise the need to rehabilitate the intellect. In Albert Einstein's words: *We cannot solve our deep problems with the same thinking that brought us these problems.*

The governments of the world must recognise their emergent obligation to develop, strengthen the intellect by reconstituting the present educational systems.

Svadharma One's Own Nature and *Paradharma* Alien Nature

Yet another important facet of education is the student's choice of his field of learning. The choice must be based on his inherent nature, innate bent known as *vasanas*. Each student, like any other human being, has distinct *vasanas* which define his individuality. From an early age the *vasanas* manifest in a student as a clear tendency, a definite inclination towards engineering or medicine, history or philosophy, painting or music etc. Such tendency, inclination arising from his *vasanas* is said to be his *svadharma*. *Sva* means 'one's own.' *Dharma* means 'nature.' A student must necessarily choose a subject in accordance with his *svadharma*. Anything alien to one's own nature is called *paradharma*. *Para* means 'alien' and *dharma*, 'nature.' It is important for a student to follow his *svadharma* and avoid *paradharma*. His life's course would then be smooth, progressive. If however he chooses a course which is *paradharma*, his passage in life would be rugged, retarded. *Svadharma* activity in one's life acts like a tailwind to an aircraft while *paradharma*, as headwind. Not realising this, people make the mistake of choosing a *paradharma* course.

Guardians have a tendency to push their children, wards into their business or profession regardless of each one's basic nature. It may be initially convenient for one to toe the line of the family or circumstance. But later one faces a series of problems. One could develop a monotony, boredom in continuing a *paradharma* course. It would also impair success and progress in the course.

Parents and teachers have a duty and responsibility to help students locate each one's individual nature and talent, *svadharma* at an early age. Thereafter encourage them to pursue that particular line. The educational institutions must play a significant role in this exercise.

Study Time

Study, reflection, writing and more particularly contemplation and meditation are best accomplished in the early hours of the morning between 4 am and 6 am. It is known as *sattvik* time. *Sattva* is one of the three mental temperaments that every human being is composed of. The three temperaments are:

Tamas   Inactive
Rajas   Active
Sattva Trans-active.

Tamas is the state of thoughts in inertia. When the mind is lethargic, indolent, indifferent. Indisposed to activity. A mood of sloth and sleep. Lacking intellectual or emotional manifestation. A person replete with *tamas* lives a dull, inactive life with hardly any response to the world.

Rajas is the state of passionate and agitated thoughts. When a person is rushing, hurrying, worrying with desire-ridden activities. And is attached and involved in the affairs of the world.

Sattva is the state of mind in equanimity, serenity. When a person remains poised, mature, contemplative and objective. Detached from worldly involvement and excitement.

Sattva, *rajas* and *tamas* composed in different proportions accounts for the heterogeneous variety of human beings. It is the proportion of their combination that makes humans distinct and different from one another.

The law of nature is that *sattva*, the *sattvik* nature of a person, surfaces early in the morning between 4 am and 6 am. His *rajas* and *tamas* lie low in that period. After the *sattvik* time is over, *rajas* rises to the surface while the other two remain dormant. *Rajas* predominates during the day from 6 am to 6 pm. And *tamas* props up at night from 6 pm to 4 am. The law holds good for one and all.

The law is apparent in the behaviour of human beings. Below are a few excerpts of the behavioural patterns of the three temperaments. Which should give an idea of how they influence human lives.

Whatever be the content of *sattva* in a person it manifests in the early hours. When he is more composed, thoughtful and objective. Even at the emotional level he displays affection in the early hours as opposed to lust during night-time. And when a person has more of *sattva* in him he is prone to waking up early. Furthermore, when *sattva* is predominantly high it would force him out of bed by 4 am. This is a natural phenomenon.

Likewise, the *rajas* in a person shows up during daytime between 6 am and 6 pm. The more the *rajas* the more his agitations. A predominantly *rajasik* person runs around all day in frenzied activities.

And *tamas* is seen glaringly at night. Sensual indulgences and other irresponsible, heedless activities flourish at night-time. Even a talented drunkard prefers to have his drink after sundown and not early in the morning. Gambling and other nefarious activities go late into the night.

Since education relates to one's *sattvik* temperament it would produce the best results if undertaken as early in the day as possible. Individual reflection and assimilation must necessarily fit in between 4 am and 6 am. That cannot be relegated to any other time. The idea may sound revolutionary but there is no other way to promote true education. The solution would be to implement the idea gradually in stages.

Essential Educational Material

Students need to be liberally educated in mathematics, science, classical literature and Vedanta philosophy. That would enable them develop a strong intellect. The educational authorities should provide and promote these subjects in schools and universities. And ensure a minimum level of proficiency in them is acquired by the students without violating their *svadharma* choices of study.

After considerable research the author has set up a three-year residential course at the Vedanta Academy in India for the development of the human intellect. However, for those who are not able to avail of the course he recommends a graduated study of his books:

1. *The Fall of the Human Intellect*
2. *Select English Poems*
3. *The Eternities: Vedanta Treatise.*

CHAPTER VIII

CONSEQUENCES OF DISREGARDING INTELLECT

Humanity has long disregarded the intellect. People have denied themselves the ability to think, reason independently. That has rendered humans helpless victims of the devastating mind. The once sovereign state of human beings has fallen into abject slavery to the mind's endless desires and demands. The loss of intellect has resulted in not just the slavery but far more serious consequences. People are unable to fend themselves against attractions, temptations and challenges of the external world. They strive and struggle for life in the quagmire of mundane problems and pressures. The world has turned into a veritable hell plunging humanity into stress, suffering and sorrow. The total neglect of the human intellect has caused this precipitous fall.

William Shakespeare portrays this deplorable state in his play *Othello*. He characterises the general in the army, Othello as one who has lost his intellect completely. Whose deadly emotions of attachment, jealousy, hatred have eclipsed his reason and judgement. Othello suspected his most faithful wife, Desdemona of infidelity. Ironically, Desdemona is known and accepted as Shakespeare's noblest feminine character. She is a picture of beauty, virtue and of the most charitable disposition. But the loss of intellect turned Othello blind to her divine nature. His mind tormented him with pernicious thoughts of doubt and distress about her morality. His emotions drove him raving mad. And he met the tragic end of killing his wife and himself.

Othello is just an example of the dire consequences of disregarding intellect, the vital equipment that a human being is endowed with. Several savants and sages have written valuable literature highlighting the importance of the human intellect and the devastating effects of neglecting its development and use in life. To conceive the damage, just imagine a drunken driver at the steering wheel of a vehicle moving at high speed in a highway!

The effects of neglecting the intellect and its guidance in life's activities range from a mere disconcert to destruction. As the power of the intellect diminishes in a person his mind takes over his personality. Which results in considerable damage to the person and society. Listed below are a series of repercussions caused by a neglected intellect.

Mind loses its Sanity

Without the guidance of the intellect the mind fluctuates between moods and throws up tantrums. If this continues the supportless mind would lead a person to virtual insanity.

When the mind's feeling, emotion, like and dislike drives an action without the supervision, guidance of the intellect, then that action is said to be *impulsive.* And when the intellect reasons, judges the impulse of the mind and decides on an action, it is termed *discriminative.* Discriminative actions determine the sanity of a person. As impulsive actions displace discriminative actions one loses one's sanity. The figure below shows the loss of intellect resulting in the gradual deterioration of a human being.

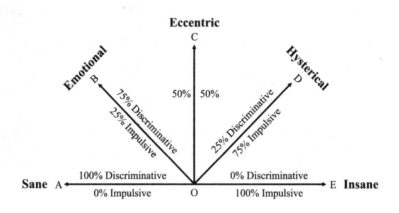

When a person uses his intellect to supervise and guide every like and dislike, feeling and emotion of the mind, his actions are 100% discriminative and 0% impulsive. He goes along OA. He is said to be a perfectly *sane* individual. As the application of his intellect reduces and discriminative actions fall to say 75% while his impulsive actions cover 25% of his actions, as in position OB, he is said to be an *emotional* person. With a further loss of intellect to around 50%, when his mind and intellect alternatively govern the personality, he moves to OC, becomes *eccentric*. And when his intellect's participation falls to around 25% and his mind takes over 75% of the behavioural pattern as in OD, he turns *hysterical*. In the last state of human deterioration, along OE, when his intellect does not function at all and the impulses of his mind rule the personality, he becomes *insane*. A careful scrutiny of the world would reveal that the present state of humanity seems to range between *emotional* and *eccentric*. That would mean considerable loss in the application of the intellect among humans.

Mind becomes Destructive

The nature of the mind is akin to that of the wind. Both are restless, turbulent, strong and obstinate.

Restless: Restless winds blow in all directions in the sky. So too a mind disturbed with uncontrolled desires runs helter-skelter in the world trying to fulfil them.

Turbulent: Turbulent winds uproot trees on land and wreck ships at sea. Similarly, when passions rise to giddy heights without intellectual surveillance and guidance, the mind could become turbulent, violent. Such minds can cause heinous crimes like rape, murder, terrorism etc.

Strong: Both wind and mind are insubstantial, yet very strong. Not concrete in form but powerful. Typhoons and tornadoes devastate buildings and bridges, wipe out villages and towns. Just so, a single person's mind can change that of an entire mob, the destiny of a nation.

Obstinate: Like the wind, the mind can be obstinate, unyielding. Wind finds its own direction. If its pursuit is hindered by any obstacle, it will force its way in another direction. The mind has a similar tendency. It relentlessly tries to fulfil its desires. And if there is any barrier obstructing its course, it will circumvent it and do all it can to reach its desired object.

Choice of Action goes Wrong

When the mind operates without the help of the intellect, the choice of action could go wrong and impair your life. The mind operates on likes and dislikes. It has the tendency to pick up what it likes and discard what it dislikes. But what is delightful in the beginning turns out to be detrimental in the end. And vice versa. What is detestable to start with ends in being beneficial. It is a natural law governing one and all. Human beings disregard this law of life. They indiscriminately choose what they like and avoid what they dislike and suffer the consequences thereof the rest of their lives.

You need a powerful intellect to control and direct your likes and dislikes, your attractions and aversions properly. *Your likes and dislikes are not to be suppressed, stifled or strangled. Your intellect has only to examine and deal with them appropriately to ensure your life runs smooth. A human can ill afford to let the whim and fancy of the mind take over his personality.* That would be catastrophic. Interestingly all other creatures, being denied the intellect, are free from the dilemma of choice.

The Herd Instinct

Another serious consequence of ignoring the intellect's role in life is one's submission to the herd instinct. People all over the world blindly follow the routine of their predecessors or mere peer pressure. You accept and do what others have done in the past or what they do at present. Without the least concern over its merits or demerits. You mechanically go through school and university, marriage and family, politics and religion. In fact you run through your life's course without questioning, enquiring the meaning and purpose of it all. The intellect hardly plays a part in the pursuit of life. Leading you to a state of confusion and chaos.

Attachment and Desire

The absence of intellectual surveillance allows thoughts to run on their own towards the external world. When your thoughts flow indiscriminately towards an object or being you develop an *attachment* for that object or being. And if the thought-flow is not checked by a discerning intellect it forms a thicker stream of thoughts in the same direction. Thoughts in that frequency turn into a *desire* for possessing and enjoying that object or being. Thus the negligence of the intellect produces endless desires in you. As long as attachment lasts and desires remain unfulfilled, your mind will be agitated. And mental agitations produce stress and strain in life.

With further negligence of the intellect, there would be no control over desires accumulated in the mind. And when your intellect has no hold on desires, the mind indulges in them freely. Such indulgence would lead you to addictions. You become a chain-smoker, an alcoholic or a drug addict. These are but a few examples of several human weaknesses that an ungoverned mind can cause.

A mind replete with desires causes problems. If your desires are thwarted and not fulfilled, you suffer frustration, bitterness, anger. If fulfilled, you indulge further and succumb to addictions. Either way, your mind denied intellectual guidance reaches a dreadful state threatening suicide, homicide, even genocide.

Ego and Complexes

Another outcome of disregarding and neglecting the intellect is emergence of the ego. A person develops an ego when his intellect fails to recognise the wonderful plan of nature that supports the world. The universe is a composite whole of the animate and inanimate. The manifold parts of nature are orchestrated to bring about the melody of existence. Every one of them has a distinct role to play. They serve as spokes in the wheel of life. None is superior or inferior. But people have not developed the intellect to perceive the perfectly designed universe. As a result of this blindness they have assumed an individual importance. They substitute their ego where nature plays its part in holding the world together. The consequent ego suffers from either a superiority or an inferiority complex.

A human being must develop his intellect to dissolve his egoistic feelings. He must learn to play his role in the general scheme of nature to the best of his ability and move on. And try to follow the brilliant observation of William Shakespeare:

All the world's a stage,
And all the men and women merely players;
They have their exits and their entrances.

109

The American philosopher-poet Ralph Waldo Emerson ridicules the complexes of a human being in his beautiful poem *The Mountain and the Squirrel*. In the poem, the mountain brags to a squirrel about its ability to carry forests on its back. The squirrel admits it does not have the enormous strength of the mountain and quips, "If I cannot carry forests on my back, neither can you crack a nut!" With all its strength the mountain cannot crack a nut. While the squirrel can with ease crack a nut but cannot manage to carry even a stone on its back. Such is the world. Constituted of diverse talents. Why develop an attitude of superiority or inferiority?

Thus an arrogant claim to superiority is as absurd as a despondent feeling of inferiority. Why have any complex? It only causes mental agitation and suffering. Hence learn to accept yourself as you are. Everyone has a distinct place and purpose in this world. None is big or small. Important or unimportant. Understand that. Live by it. You will then be free from the menace of complexes.

Success and Achievement Affected

To be successful in this competitive world, to be an achiever in any field of endeavour you would need a powerful intellect. If your intellect is neglected and weak, you would have to compensate by striving hard to make a living. A fact apparent in the world. Like animals without an intellect having to put in constant effort for their survival. They cannot afford to be lackadaisical. This is the price they pay for being denied the intellect. Even among humans, those who lack intellectual prowess will have to put in hard labour as opposed to intellectuals occupying higher cadres of management. And to become an exceptional achiever one must possess an extraordinary intellect.

Effect on Religion

The lack of intellectual development has resulted in the debacle of religions the world over. Which has caused the loss of ethics and morality. And people have turned utterly self-centred, selfish in their lives. Life today is all take, take and take. In the glorious past, it was give, give and give. In Victor Hugo's book *Les Miserables* a priest sermonises: *Life is to give, not to take*. Nature has ever been benevolent to humanity. But people are least aware of what they receive in life. With no thought of repayment. Do you realise that the day you were born you were provided with oxygen, mother's milk, the right temperature and pressure in your body, the right temperature and pressure in your environment, a million more — all for your survival. Through your lifetime the world has provided you with food, water, endless gifts. But human selfishness is so intense that none seem to be even aware, much less grateful to the benevolence lavished on humanity. Prophet Mohammed makes a striking observation: *He is best among human beings who is best at repaying.*

The fall of the intellect has turned religion into a mockery. One section of people hawks spirituality with its own views. Another section blindly accepts them. Religion has deteriorated to mere parroting of ideas by preachers and blind acceptance by followers. Neither teacher nor taught go through a systematic process of study, reflection and contemplation on the spiritual truths. The blind leads the blind. There is no thought or reason backing present-day religious practices. And the world remains poor spiritually and morally. As a result people are warring with each other. Going through suffering and misery.

Study the series of repercussions enumerated above. Examine their relevance to your personality. And attend to the areas applicable to you. Correct them where necessary. You need to develop and use your intellect to achieve this.

CHAPTER IX

WHAT PAUCITY OF INTELLECT CREATES

For generations humans have been ignorant of the value and importance of the intellect. Their ignorance has led to total indifference and neglect of this vital equipment. As a result the human intellect has remained emaciated, weak. People in the world today operate with a defunct intellect. And are unaware that they are confused and confounded with regard to actions and relations in their lives. People have no clear concept of what they want and what they do in this world. The American humorist and writer, Mark Twain remarks: *The perfection of wisdom and the end of true philosophy is to proportion our wants to our possessions, our ambitions to our capacities, we will then be a happy and a virtuous people.*

Below is a general coverage of the human faults in dealing with the fundamental issues governing life. What the paucity of intellect has created. An examination and analysis of each of them should help you realise any errors in judgement and correct them.

Freedom and Bondage

You need a sharp intellect to conceive the true nature of freedom. People are dependent upon the objects and beings of the world. Bound to them in all ways and claim to be free. The body and its senses constantly run after sensual pleasures. The mind craves for emotional satisfaction. The intellect never stops its quest for information and knowledge. Every human being succumbs to the never-ending demands of his body, mind and intellect. Thus people are slaves to their own passions. Stuck to WEB-site, inter-NET or CELL-phone. People are caught up in a web, net or cell all through life and claim to be free! Your intellect must study your present state and work toward true freedom. Gain self-sufficiency in every facet of life. Humans alone can achieve this status.

Richness and Poverty

Richness and poverty is not determined by the quantum of wealth one possesses. People having abundant wealth feel they are poor. Vice versa. Those with meagre means consider themselves quite rich. The English poet Oliver Goldsmith in his poem *The Village Preacher* gives the profile of an exceptional preacher. Goldsmith describes him as a man *passing rich with forty pounds a year*. You need a clear intellect to interpret rich and poor as a subject of the mind.

Richness and poverty is actually determined by the equation between the wealth a person possesses and the desires he entertains. If his desires are contained within the level of his wealth he would be a rich person. If on the contrary, his desires exceed the quantum of his wealth he would be poor.

Desires less than Wealth = Richness

Desires more than Wealth = Poverty

The masses are unaware of this equation. Innocent as they are, they invest all their time and effort in merely acquiring more and more wealth. They do not care to check the desires multiplying and rising above the quanta acquired. With the desires overtaking their wealth the tireless acquirers of wealth remain ever poor.

A person possessing a strong intellect acts cautiously to keep his desires contained within the wealth acquired. He remains rich regardless of the quantum he possesses.

Health and Ill health

A feeble intellect is carried away by the looks of health rather than sound health. Many appear healthy and believe to be so while they are far from it. The modern era lacks the penetration of thought in practically every facet of life. So it is with physical health. Just as vegetables are fertilized to appear good, so are physical bodies boosted with supplements and vitamins. For mere looks. You need a deeper insight to learn and understand the difference between health and ill health. Use your intellect to programme proper food intake and exercise to maintain perfect health all through your life. You will then realise even aging is a myth.

Love and Attachment

Another blunder in intellectual judgement is the failure to distinguish love from attachment. People everywhere believe that they possess love. Few understand the meaning and magnitude of love. Love is being in harmony with one and all. Realising your identity with living beings. A feeling that helps you live in peace and bliss. If you lack the feeling of oneness, consider yourself distinct and separate from the rest, you fall out of harmony with the world. And live in suffering and sorrow. Today the concept of love has been totally distorted. What people claim as love is personal, preferential attachment. When love is polluted by selfishness it turns sour, becomes attachment. Attachment therefore is perversion of love.

The modern world is bereft of love. Instead there is a holocaust of attachment everywhere. The great writer-poet Oliver Goldsmith endorses this staggering truth in his book *The Vicar of Wakefield*:

> *And what is friendship but a name,*
> *A charm that lulls to sleep;*
> *A shade that follows wealth or fame,*
> *But leaves the wretch to weep?*

> *And love is still an emptier sound,*
> *The modern fair one's jest:*
> *On earth unseen, or only found*
> *To warm the turtle's nest.*

All humanity suffers from the slings and arrows of the outrageous passion of attachment. The human intellect at present is so weak that it does not recognise the deadly nature of attachment. And reduces the beautiful face of love to an ugly caricature.

Knowledge and Wisdom

Knowledge must be distinguished from wisdom. You gain knowledge from teachers and textbooks. But wisdom you attain when your intellect reflects, contemplates upon the knowledge acquired. People who are well read, well informed invariably fail to live up to what they have learnt. They may appreciate a beautiful trait and not be able to imbibe it. They possess the knowledge but not the wisdom to live by it. One could know the highest principles of life and personally not follow them. You need a developed intellect to reflect upon the knowledge to assimilate it, absorb it. Knowledge then sublimates into wisdom. Thereafter it manifests in your thought, word and deed.

The paucity of intellect makes it difficult for one to recognise the difference between knowledge and wisdom. Much less elevate one's knowledge to the level of wisdom.

Abstinence and Enjoyment

The mass of humanity craves indulgence in external objects and beings. People indiscriminately run after sensual pleasures of the world. Few attempt to think, analyse the nature of their pursuits of enjoyment.

You need a developed intellect to understand that indulgence corrodes enjoyment. When your sense organ contacts a sense-object you experience a quantum of enjoyment. On contacting it again and again the quantum diminishes. And by repeated indulgence you gradually lose the enjoyment of that object or being. Any further contact with it does not give you the desired enjoyment. That state is called neutralisation.

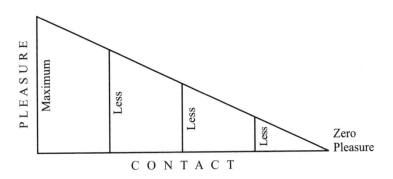

Through indulgence you become neutralised to the enjoyment of objects and beings. Indulgence actually deprives you of the enjoyment you seek from them.

Consequently, your life turns out to be insipid, monotonous in the world.

Due to the paucity of intellect people do not realise that it is through the discipline of regulated abstinence that one can really enjoy the world. Your intellect must constantly check and control indiscriminate indulgence. And discreetly refrain from and regulate your sensual activities. With such discipline you can maintain the level of your enjoyment all through life.

Mundane and Spiritual

Deprived of a clear intellect people have a distorted view of what is mundane and what is spiritual. They err in basing their views on non-essentials to determine the difference. They rely on external factors like one's station, vocation, erudition, outward behaviour or other. Few realise that these non-essentials bear no relevance to materiality or spirituality.

You need a sound intellect to determine who is mundane or spiritual. A spiritual person is one who has offloaded his desires and developed a sense of dispassion towards the world. His interest and attention has shifted from the terrestrial to the

Transcendental. He has no value for anything that the world offers. He revels in the supreme Reality, the substratum of all that exists. Becomes self-sufficient. And remains ever peaceful and blissful.

Whereas the materialist is one who entertains a value for anything in the world. He is replete with desires and lost in his life trying to fulfil them. The unfulfilled desires keep him stressful through his lifetime. Shattering him with worry and anxiety.

A deficient intellect attributes spirituality to a person for strange reasons. It projects a person to be spiritual just because of the position he holds, the robes he wears, the scriptural texts he has memorised or the reclusive life he leads. None of these nor other non-essentials can confer spiritual status on him.

The tragic misconception of spirituality has led to the chaos and confusion of religious sects, creeds and denominations. In the name of religion human beings have broken up into various divisions and demarcations. It has resulted in intolerance, bitterness and animosity among religious bodies and persons. Breeding militancy, terrorism and wars. This situation threatening the world today has emanated from sheer negligence of the intellect.

The loss of intellect has turned cancerous to the human society. It has caused immense damage to humans in every facet of their lives. A person with a dull intellect is confused as to his role in the world. He fails to perform his obligatory duties and responsibilities. And when his intellect deteriorates to the extreme, when reason and discretion is fully shrouded, he sees things perverted. Even regards unrighteousness as righteousness, vice as virtue. Such people consider massacring humans or animals as just. The absence of intellect has led to such atrocities.

You must therefore carefully study all the errors in judgement enunciated in this chapter. Find out those areas which relate to your personality and correct them. A developed intellect should help you achieve this.

CHAPTER X

WAKE UP, SAVE THE WORLD

Two Types of Intellect

There are two types of intellect known as *tikshna buddhi* gross-intellect and *sukshma buddhi* subtle-intellect. They play distinct roles in human life. The foregoing chapters dealt with the nature and function of the gross-intellect alone.

The gross-intellect has a wide application in the world and a valuable part to play in human life. It explores and investigates, discovers and invents endless artifices and contrivances, amenities and facilities, ways and means for bettering the standard of living in the planet.

Its application ranges from the simplest discrimination between day and night to the highest scientific discoveries and inventions. Nevertheless, the gross-intellect can operate only within the periphery of the terrestrial world. That is its limitation. It lacks the potential to go beyond the terrestrial and explore the Transcendental. That should explain why brilliant scientists, possessing the most powerful gross-intellects, are unable to unravel the mystery of the unknown Reality.

The universe is a phenomenon of cause and effect. Seed produces tree, tree produces seed. Chicken produces egg, egg produces chicken. The law of cause and effect pervades the microcosm and the macrocosm. The gross-intellect is perennially engaged in discovering numberless laws within the extremities of the universe. But it cannot discover the very cause of the universe itself. The subtle-intellect alone can conceive and explore beyond those extremities. One would need a powerful subtle-intellect to reach the transcendental State.

Every human being possesses a definite proportion of the gross and subtle-intellects. There are people with a powerful gross-intellect and a weak subtle-intellect. Others with a powerful subtle-intellect who have not applied themselves to develop their gross-intellect. However, the functions of the two intellects cannot be interchanged. One cannot be substituted for the other. Like spanners used for repairing automobiles and wristwatches. An automobile spanner cannot be used to fix a wristwatch. Nor a wristwatch spanner be used to fix the nuts and bolts of an automobile. Their functions are distinct and apart from one another.

Thus a person with the most powerful gross-intellect, like a scientist, finds it difficult to conceive the transcendental Reality, much less comprehend It. While the spiritually evolved, with a well-developed subtle-intellect, has neither interest nor enthusiasm to deal with anything terrestrial. The mass of humanity possesses a gross-intellect of varying strengths but hardly any subtle-intellect. People do not realise that the beauty and grandeur of a human being lies in the possession of a sound subtle-intellect. Which alone can transport one to the unknown state of Enlightenment. While the gross-intellect plies between the known states of the waking, dream and deep-sleep.

Waker, Dreamer, Deep-Sleeper and Self

Every human being goes through the three states of consciousness — waking, dream and deep-sleep. The gross-intellect is unaware of anything beyond these three states. It sees the entire human life revolving perennially around the waker, dreamer and deep-sleeper. It is important to study them carefully. Examine and analyse them one by one.

The waker in the waking state refers to himself as **I**. So does the dreamer in the dream state declare himself as **I**. And the deep-sleeper as **I**. The waker, dreamer and deep-sleeper are different and distinct personalities. How can they all be the same **I**? There lies the mystery: Who is this **I**?

In the waking state the waker declares, "I am an athlete." In the dream the dreamer says, "I am an invalid." And in deep-sleep the deep-sleeper, "I am blank, nothing." The athlete cannot be the invalid and both cannot be nothing. They are three different personalities. How can three unequal factors be equal to one single factor **I**? The staggering truth is that **I** has to be different from the athlete, invalid and nothing. Therefore **I** cannot be the athlete, invalid and nothing. **I** cannot be the waker, the dreamer or the deep-sleeper. What, who then is this mysterious **I**?

Who is **I**?

The problem is that the world comprises only wakers, dreamers and deep-sleepers. Every one of them freely refers to one's personality as **I**. Like the waker above declares, "I am an athlete." But this is not true. Think carefully. The I is not the athlete. The 'waker' is the athlete. That is the truth. Then who is I?

Likewise the dreamer and deep-sleeper commit the same error. The I therefore is not the invalid or nothing. The grievous problem is that the I is at all times flavoured as the waker, dreamer or deep-sleeper. The I is never experienced as I, the real Self. Imagine water at all times knowing itself as Coke, Pepsi or Fanta and never as pure water. Similarly, I always knows Itself as the three flavoured personalities of the athlete, invalid, nothing. As the waker, dreamer, deep-sleeper life after life. And never as the true I, the real Self. Herein lies the mystery of the Unknown: Who is I?

Who am I?

Now carefully study the following observations.

1. The child declares, "I am a child." Growing up the boy declares, "I am a boy." Later, "I am an adult." Much later, "I am an old person." The child, boy, adult, old person are all different. But they are all equated to I.

2. A person using the organs of action states, "I act." The same person using the organs of perception states,

"I see, I hear, I smell, I taste, I touch." Using the mind, "I feel emotions." And with the intellect, "I think, I contemplate." But acting, perceiving, feeling, thinking and contemplating are distinct and different experiences. Yet all of them are equated to I.

3. The waker, dreamer and deep-sleeper independently declare, "I am an athlete," "I am an invalid," "I am nothing" respectively. Three different personalities — athlete, invalid, nothing — are equated to I.

The above observations reveal that I pervades the entire life from childhood to old age. I pervades all physical, mental and intellectual experiences. I pervades the waking, dream and deep-sleep states. Thus, I exists as the most constant factor in every experience, everything, everywhere, every moment. In effect, the I is seen as the supreme Self reflecting omnipotence, omniscience, omnipresence, eternity. These are declared as the divine attributes of the transcendental Reality, referred to as God. A powerful subtle-intellect alone can come to know and realise the real I, the Self within.

The scriptures have declared in no uncertain terms that the Self is the supreme Reality.

Old Testament : The Voice of God declares, "I am that I am."

New Testament : Jesus Christ affirms, "The kingdom of God is within you."

Quran : Prophet Mohammed asserts, "The greatest jihad is that for the conquest of Self."

Bhagavad Gita : Krishna pronounces, "I am the Self in all beings."

Upanishads : The Rishis (Enlightened Sages) avow, "Self is God."

Your real Self is absolute peace and bliss. That is your original Being. You have lost the status of your Self. Descended to the material layers identifying with your body, mind and intellect. And now you are possessed with desires to find your lost happiness through these equipments. The pressure of desires never ceases until you find your original Self. In truth, the purpose of human birth is to regain one's primal nature.

Absolute peace and happiness lies within one's Self. Yet people are rushing all over to find it in the world. None has succeeded in finding it through external pursuits. The mad rush goes on. Not realising one's original being is the Self. Arthur Schopenhauer, the German philosopher, wisely advises all human beings: *It is difficult to find happiness within oneself but it is impossible to find it anywhere else.*

Here are two simple experiments to demonstrate that Self is the original Being:

1. Place a coil spring four feet high on a table. Press it down with your palm to one foot. The pressure built in pushes your palm upward. Release it to two feet. The pressure reduces. Release it to three feet. The pressure reduces further. Release it to four feet. There is no pressure at all because it has reached its original state.

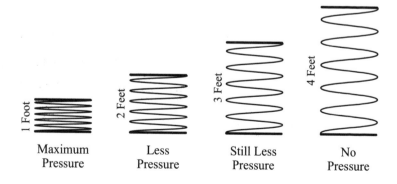

| Maximum Pressure | Less Pressure | Still Less Pressure | No Pressure |

2. Hold a straight cane at its ends with both your hands. Bend it to form an arc. There is a pressure to straighten itself. Release it a little. The pressure reduces. Release it gradually till it becomes straight. Then there is no pressure at all because it has reached its original state.

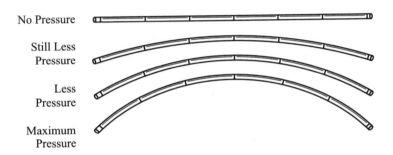

No Pressure

Still Less Pressure

Less Pressure

Maximum Pressure

In these experiments, both the spring and cane develop pressures no sooner they lose their original forms. And the pressure builds up as they recede from their origin. Conversely, the pressure reduces as they move towards it. And ceases on regaining their original states.

Likewise, desires incessantly pressurise humans to gain more and more peace and happiness. The pursuit goes on throughout their lifetime. The pressure of desires ends only on realising the all-blissful Self. Self-realised Souls bear testimony to this truth. Hence, the Self is declared to be your original Being.

The Self speaks through your eyes and ears, through your feeling and emotion, through your thought, word and deed. It remains ever so close and dear to you. And yet you speak eloquently of everything except your true Being. The American philosopher Ralph Waldo Emerson deplores the ignorant state of humans when he states: *Who you are speaks so loudly, I can't understand what you are saying.*

Your Role in the Revival

Study this literature in detail. You would then realise the predicament of beings in this planet. Brought about by the total neglect and the consequent fall of the human intellect. It is now the obligation, duty and responsibility of the few who have understood the situation to resurrect the fallen intellect. As a consequence of this blunder the human race has become an endangered species.

Every human must realise this grave situation and rehabilitate the intellect. Start the process with thinking, enquiring at every facet of life. You ought not to take anything for granted. Think, examine whatever you meet in life and accept only those that stand to reason. This discipline should have been initiated to everyone at the age of six or seven years. Had it been implemented from the very beginning, the impending disaster could have been averted. But humanity has failed to do so. To compensate for it now the effort in rehabilitation has to be increased a hundredfold. The procedure for rehabilitation of the intellect needs to be undertaken by the individual, by the society and educational institutions throughout the world.

The process consists of two daily practices.

1. *To develop the intellect:* One must study the author's three books in the order of:

   i.   *The Fall of the Human Intellect*
   ii. *Select English Poems*
   iii. *The Eternities: Vedanta Treatise.*

This exercise needs to be followed daily in the early hours of the morning as close to 4 am as possible.

2. *Make use of the existing intellect:* The problem among humans is that they do not make use of their existing intellect fully. That explains why people

regret their own actions. This can be solved by the practice of introspection. Introspection is a process of self-observation. To be practised every night before you retire. It involves the recollection of your experiences during the day. Try and remember every experience you have gone through in a sequence from the time of rising to the moment of introspecting. In your initial attempts you may not remember the details of what you have done. But with repeated practice you will recollect each and every activity. This exercise should not take you more than five to six minutes. While practising introspection do not analyse or criticise your actions. You are only to be aware of them. Do not get involved in the merit or demerit of the action. That would break the trend of introspection. Moreover, it may develop cynicism and frustration. When you remember an action over and over again you become aware of it. And constant recollection of daily actions would render your existing intellect alert.

Therefore

The residual thinkers in the world must plunge into a massive programme to revive, rehabilitate the fallen intellect. Humanity has to realise the present state of emergency caused by the total neglect of this vital equipment. Individuals are tormented by stress, depression and disease. Nations are torn apart by vandalism, militancy and terrorism. Everywhere. Humans must wake up to this stern reality.

You are humans. You alone can do it. Save yourselves. Save the world.

INDEX

* Poem appears in the author's book
    entitled *Select English Poems.*

138

Select English Poems
3 Editions

A collection of 20 masterpieces from English literature. Includes selections from the works of William Shakespeare, Samuel Johnson, Oliver Goldsmith, John Milton, William Wordsworth and Matthew Arnold.

The book analyses each literary piece to derive the powerful messages encapsulated in classic prose and poetry. These convey the highest values of life and philosophical insights essential for enduring peace and prosperity.

The Eternities: Vedanta Treatise
14 Editions - Bestseller

The Vedanta Treatise expounds the ancient philosophy of the Vedas. It presents the eternal principles of life and living. Living is a technique that needs to be learnt and practised. The technique provides the formula for combining continual action with enduring peace. It further equips one with a clear intellect to meet the challenges of the world.

Above all, the Treatise helps one evolve to greater heights on the spiritual path. It provides the knowledge and guidance to reach the ultimate in human perfection. The goal of Self-realisation.